LADDER

CLIMBING OUT OF A SLUMP

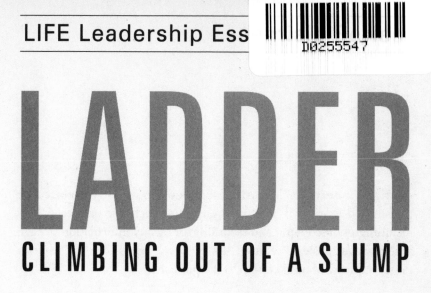

NEVER LET A GOOD SLUMP
GO TO WASTE!

FOREWORD BY

DAN HAWKINS

OBSTACLES
PRESS

First Edition, May 2015
10 9 8 7 6 5 4 3 2 1

Published by:

Obstaclés Press
200 Commonwealth Court
Cary, NC 27511

lifeleadership.com

ISBN: 978-0-9961843-4-2

Cover design and layout by Norm Williams, nwa-inc.com

Printed in the United States of America

The best place to wait out a hailstorm
is under a portico filled with violin music.
—CHRIS BRADY, *A MONTH OF ITALY*

CONTENTS

FOREWORD

by Dan Hawkins

In any endeavor, there will be ups and downs, peaks and valleys, good times and bad. Life is filled with surprises that will knock you off your game. There seems to be a common misconception that those who have succeeded had it easy, had fewer obstacles, or were even just lucky. That could not be further from the truth. Many times, those with the biggest wins have suffered the most crushing losses.

Michael Jordan was once quoted as saying, "I've missed more than 9,000 shots in my career. I've lost almost 300 games. Twenty-six times, I've been trusted to take the game-winning shot and missed. I've failed over and over and over again in my life. And that is why I succeed."

What seems to set those who truly succeed apart from the masses is the ability to miss shots but continue shooting, to fall down but get back up. No matter what the challenge is, setbacks can always be expected. If you study people who have made it to the top in anything from sports to business, you will find stories of overcoming great odds, from facing critics that are so harsh just reading about them makes you cringe to surmounting obstacles that make what you are going through seem very small and insignificant.

Stories of success are very similar in the process but different in the details. Every story worth hearing follows the sequence: Dream, Struggle, Victory. The story you are writing right now, even as you read this book, will follow the same path. Leadership expert Orrin Woodward says, "Everyone gets knocked down. Winners get back up." The question you need to ask yourself is: Will I *give up* in the struggle, or will I *grow up* in the struggle?

Studying the practices and thinking of successful people reveals that they all share some common traits. *Ladder: Climbing Out of a Slump* explains these thought processes and practices as well as how to apply them to your own journey of success. This book will help you recognize when you are in a slump and give you the tools to climb back out. And as you do, you will become better and progress even higher than your previous climb. You will learn how to enjoy the valleys because they give you a new perspective of the peaks and priceless lessons for the next climb. A big part of becoming a success is enjoying this process.

You, my friend, are headed for some exciting times. By reading this book, you have already proven you are a force to be reckoned with, a Rascal, as bestselling author Chris Brady would say. However, having the right information and process is only the beginning. Just by learning how to climb out of a slump, you are by definition inviting the slump into your path. But remember, this is the path of every champion, and you are well on your way. All you need to do is muster the will to win, ignore unhelpful criticism, and push through your doubts, fears, and obstacles. Get up, look up, and begin your climb.

These are the moments when you begin to win and create the stories you will one day share with others who decide to take the path less traveled. The memories you will be most proud of will happen in this process.

Whether you are in a slump now or just know one is coming, I pray you take the wisdom from this book and become an example, a hero that others around you need, so one day they will have the courage to climb with you.

Dan Hawkins
Cofounder of LIFE Leadership

INTRODUCTION

It is a truth universally acknowledged…
—JANE AUSTEN, *PRIDE AND PREJUDICE*

Sometimes the most important lessons are passed down to future generations in clichés, proverbs, or maxims. In fact, only the most lasting ideas, the proven principles, the most obvious truisms, stay around long enough to become so traditional that they are repeated over and over. Ironically, it is at this point that most people stop listening to them.

But there is another group of people, great leaders, who realize that success and progress are the natural consequences of learning true principles and tenaciously applying them against opposition, roadblocks, criticism, and all the odds. Great leaders do the little things, the basics, the most important things, and they do them consistently. They get passionate about mastering the simple little habits that bring about nearly all success in the world. As C. S. Lewis

> **Great leaders do the little things, the basics, the most important things, and they do them consistently.**

taught, this makes them the "master craftsmen" of their field, their sector, their business.[1]

While the masses, what we might symbolically call "the 95 percent," are content not to achieve this level, "the 5 percent" reach for a higher plane. These are the real leaders in the world.

The simple but key things they learn to master include the foundations of success such as hard work, attention to detail, faith and loyalty even in the face of ridicule, frugality even in a world that embraces debt and extravagance, honesty and integrity, taking care of one's colleagues and customers, innovating when things get hard, and turning lemons into lemonade. When the going gets tough, the tough get going. Cliché, yes. But true. And real. As business leader and *New York Times* bestselling author Chris Brady put it: "Every now and then, a strong storm is good for the soul."[2]

What many people call the secrets of success aren't secrets at all. They're just truths. Principles. Applying them is wisdom, and those who do so consistently inevitably become great leaders — because there is real power in truth and service and the courage to do the right thing no matter what the world throws at you.

Great leaders also turn problems into opportunities, difficulties into victories, and thorns into roses. They turn lemons into lemonade, as the old saying goes, or better still, into lemon meringue pies. They turn every slump into a ladder they climb to reach new levels of success.

Great leaders are familiar with this ladder, their old friend. They bond together over tears, mud, sweat, and blood. They bond over slivers and struggles, and they smile together in the victories. Over time, these two, the leader and the Ladder, come to respect each other. When a slump comes, the Ladder knows the leader will soon return, climbing rung by rung to a better future.

At the same time, as soon as the leader realizes he or she is in a slump of any sort, the leader immediately thinks of the Ladder. The leader knows that the slump isn't the story; the climb is, as is the victory ahead.

Where most people worry, complain, blame, or at least shake their heads in frustration that a slump has come into their lives, the leader does something different. The leader smiles, knowing the Ladder is a friend and the slump is a call to something better. And the leader takes action.

Specifically, the leader climbs the Six Rungs of what we call the Slump-to-Success Ladder. As part of the 5 percent, he or she climbs in a very special way, one powerful rung at a time.

This pattern always works. It doesn't shelter anyone from the reality that slumps are a part of life or that challenges come

> **Where most people worry, complain, blame, or at least shake their heads in frustration that a slump has come into their lives, the leader does something different. The leader smiles, knowing the Ladder is a friend and the slump is a call to something better. And the leader takes action.**

to everyone, but it does something much better. It allows the leader to turn any challenge, slump, or difficulty into a stepping stone to more success and increased progress.

When you know the rungs of the Ladder and climb them consistently any time a challenge or slump comes into your life, you become part of the small group of people, the 5 percent, who are on the path of great service and great success. This is not an easy path, but it is a lot more fun than the other paths.

> **When you know the rungs of the Ladder and climb them consistently any time a challenge or slump comes into your life, you become part of the small group of people, the 5 percent, who are on the path of great service and great success.**

And, inevitably, the path of success leads to the Ladder. Slumps, challenges, difficulties, and crises will come, as they come to everyone. They'll be major roadblocks for some people, pulling them down, convincing them to give up, pushing them to settle for less than they really want from themselves and their lives. But such problems won't stop real leaders. In fact, they signal to leaders that it's time to climb the Ladder.

Those who use every slump as a simple call to climb the Ladder will naturally turn every challenge into a greater success. Whatever happens to them, they'll come out better than before. They'll progress in all eventualities. They'll adapt, innovate, and overcome, no matter the difficulties they face.

Onlookers, those in the 95 percent, will frequently call such people "lucky" or, ironically, even "selfish," but the leaders know the truth. They turn every slump into a great increase simply because they climb the Ladder. This is hard work, not luck. It requires focus, tenacity, and courage. And they do it not just for themselves but to bless the lives of many other people as well.

Those who climb the Ladder know that luck has little to do with success. Taking action when others are paralyzed by the task, yes. Faith, yes. Perseverance, yes. Putting their hand in God's and trusting as they do the right thing, yes. Loyalty, yes. Keeping both feet and their whole heart working to climb the Ladder, yes.

Two men walk into a bar.

Actually, ninety-five people walk into a bar. Five don't. They have better things to do. They are busy building something important, something that matters.

Leaders face ups and downs as often as everyone else. But over time, great leaders master the simple habit of responding to every slump by climbing the Slump-to-Success Ladder. When there are no slumps or big crises in their lives, they focus on doing important things and building their life purpose. When one does come, they redouble their Ladder climbing efforts. And

> **Over time, great leaders master the simple habit of responding to every slump by climbing the Slump-to-Success Ladder.**

this usually catapults them even more effectively toward success and progress.

Most people try to avoid slumps but get stuck in them nevertheless. Great leaders embrace slumps, and by climbing the rungs of the Ladder, they swing every slump like a pendulum to even greater success than before.

Let's learn how they do it.

WORD OF THE DAY

leader: "pioneer, frontrunner, innovator, trailblazer, ground-breaker, trendsetter, torch-bearer; originator, initiator, founder..."

(Compact Oxford Thesaurus)

*The way to handle setbacks
is persistence.*[3]
—BILL LEWIS

THE ART OF
THE SLUMP

Ask, and it will be given you…
—MATTHEW 7:7

Sooner or later, you're going to go through a slump. When you do, this book will help you take action immediately and effectively. Even more important, it will help you hurdle slumps in the first place. It will help you instantly see a slump for what it really is. It will also help you counsel and mentor other people who face slumps (and everyone does) because you'll know exactly how to overcome any slump that comes along.

Slumps are a natural part of life, so becoming adept at recognizing and overcoming them is a powerful skill. Effective leaders know how to deal with slumps. Moreover, they know something much

> **Effective leaders know something profound: how to turn any slump into a huge catalyst for major improvement.**

more profound: how to turn any slump into a huge catalyst for major improvement.

This book will teach you how to turn any and every
slump into a brief but potent period of shifting your focus,
never letting the slump last, languish, or hold you back. It
will teach you how to do this without letting the slump go
to waste—because the truth is that every slump is a great
opportunity. Slumps come for a very important reason:

They are telling you that something needs to change.

Unfortunately, most people often change the wrong
things and give up or settle for less than they want. But
those who achieve real success in their lives learn to immediately recognize and change the right things.

Indeed, a slump shouldn't be an excuse to decide to
give up, forget your dreams, change your life's upward
direction, stop striving for greatness, or stop making difficult changes. Rather, slumps should demand your conscious

> **A slump's message is to go deeper, do better, and get going!**

attention because they are actually telling you to do the
exact *opposite* of all these things. A slump's message is to
go deeper, do better, and get going! "Wake up!" a slump
yells at you. "Something big is ahead, if only you'll get
serious right now and reach for something much better!
Get to work! Make haste! Keep going! Give it your all!"

This is counterintuitive for most people because a slump almost always feels negative. But those who learn this powerful lesson experience a lot more success in life than those who don't. Slumps don't tell us to slow down or give in; they tell us to stand up and stand out!

The message of every slump includes a powerful feeling of change, but it's not the change of doing less, of eating chocolate on the couch in your pajamas, or of drowning your sorrows in a six-week, high-fructose-corn-syrup cold cereal binge. It's the

> **Slumps don't tell us to slow down or give in; they tell us to stand up and stand out!**

change of doing more and doing things better. That's what a slump is telling you, if you know how to listen. The "art of the slump" consists simply of knowing how to accurately hear the real message:

- Stand up and get going!

- Take charge of your life, forget anything that is holding you back, and simply go after your dreams with all your heart!

- Stop listening to voices that tell you things are hard or that you're not good enough. These thoughts are causing the slump, not vice versa.

- Don't avoid making changes in your life because they are difficult.

- Change more, not less! Go for what really matters to you!

- The easy things will keep you where you are, but you can do (and *be*) much better.

- Keep striving for greatness!

- Embrace the difficult things that will bring real, lasting, positive change and what you really want in life!

These are a slump's real messages that your subconscious is trying to communicate to you. If you are in a slump, copy this list and carry it with you everywhere. Read it when you first wake up in the morning, right before you go to bed, and right before every meal. It will only take you a few seconds to read, but doing so will make an enormous difference. Keep rereading and repeating this message until you fully believe it.

> **Slumps come along at key moments when you have the chance to take things to a whole new level, to succeed more than before, and to improve and overcome any mediocrity in your life.**

Slumps are powerful. Slumps are excellent. Slumps are wonderful! They come along at key moments when you have the chance to take things to a whole new level, to succeed more than before, and to improve and overcome any mediocrity in your life. Even though it might feel like their purpose is to tell you to give up, do less, stop pushing, settle for less, and lower your dreams, that's not the case; their purpose is to let you know that it's time to reach deeper and do better.

This is the art of the slump: knowing what a slump is really trying to tell you and then doing something about it, something that works, something that matters, something that changes everything and rescripts the future—*your* future.

When you know the true language of the slump, you have more power. When you know what to do when a slump hits, you have more strength. You'll be a better leader. And when you take the right steps consistently, you'll find yourself on the path of real success.

> **When you know what to do when a slump hits, you have more strength.**

In fact, when you master the art of the slump, you'll almost look forward to slumps. Really! When slumps come along, you'll grin, lick your chops, and take a deep breath. You'll instantly know that a lot of hard work is ahead because it's time to step on Rung 1 of the Slump-to-Success Ladder. And you'll immediately do so—with gusto—knowing that a big, positive success is coming.

This will bring a smile to your lips and a twinkle to your eye—but only if you know the art of the slump. If you don't, the onset of a slump will bring a groan and cause you to feel frustrated, worried, and overwhelmed.

But that's not what slumps are for! People who let slumps get them down are letting the potential of a slump go to waste. That's sad.

Moreover, it is a sure way to lessen your power, dull your wits, and diminish your leadership. It will inhibit your creativity, stifle your ingenuity, and put you on the path of decline. That's a bad place to be.

Instead, leaders learn to understand the message of a slump. They embrace any and all slumps because they know what they mean. They mean more success, pure and simple.

Yes, a slump is telling you that change is needed. But this change will drastically, quickly, and powerfully make things better. This book will teach you how to make this type of change. And once you do, many things in your life will click into place. Doors will open, opportunities will knock, relationships will improve, and success will be just a few steps up the Ladder. Will it take a lot of work? Of course it will. But so would sitting around feeling frustrated, moping and worrying, wondering what comes next, wishing life and success were just easy, and whining that you're in a rut and don't know what to do.

> **When you give in to the moping kind of slump, the results are more negativity and increased frustration.**

That's the wrong kind of work, the kind that makes things worse. When you give in to the moping kind of slump, the results are more negativity and increased frustration. Instead, do the work of climbing the Slump-to-Success Ladder. Such work brings real results, real change, and real progress. Plus, it's a lot more fun.

It may seem strange that the onset of a slump could make you chuckle with excitement and anticipation, but that is exactly what it does when you know the language and art of the slump.

Have you ever wondered if the top leaders you admire have some special secret, some hidden knowledge that brings them increased success, no matter what difficulties, challenges, or roadblocks come along? The truth is that such knowledge isn't hidden. Rather, it's totally out in the open. Unfortunately, most people just don't believe it or act on it. That's the difference between great leaders and the rest of the people: great leaders act on the basics, the fundamental principles and habits of success. That's the secret of the 5 percent.

They know that difficulties are supposed to bring out the best in us, so when challenges come, they do something amazing: they smile, ignore negative "what ifs," and focus on what really matters. These are simple, well-known principles that are taught far

> **Top leaders do the little things because they have faith, and they take action to apply true principles.**

and wide. But most people don't apply them.

Leaders do. That's the great "secret," the "hidden knowledge" of huge success. Top leaders do the little things because they have faith, and they take action to apply true principles. That's the only great secret of success. And it's no secret.

The simple reality is when you apply true principles, good things happen. When you don't, not as many good things come along.

So when you find that you have entered a slump or rut in your life, you can take the road of the 95 percent and let negative feelings, thoughts, and anxieties get you down, or you can choose to be part of the 5 percent and make a different decision. You can choose to smile widely, beam with anticipation, and say, "Wow! I'm in a slump. This is wonderful. This is fabulous. It's about time. I can't wait to go to the next level!"

> **The simple reality is when you apply true principles, good things happen. When you don't, not as many good things come along.**

Then you can immediately take the first step, lifting yourself to Rung 1 of the Slump-to-Success Ladder. And over the next few days, you can climb the other rungs of the Ladder as well, one at a time.

If you do this — despite the fact that most people take a different path — you'll turn any slump into a stepladder to more success. You'll promptly put your faith in truth and true principles, and at the same time, you'll firmly choose focus and action. And this will make all the difference.

As Robert Frost wrote:

Two roads diverged in a wood, and I—
I took the one less traveled by,
And that has made all the difference.[4]

WORD OF THE DAY

maxim: "saying, adage, aphorism, proverb, motto…, axiom…, dictum, precept, epigram; truism, cliché."

(Compact Oxford Thesaurus)

I can tell I'm in a slump when I start watching more news....If you want to pull out of a slump, you're going to have to protect your attitude....You have to watch who you hang out with.[5]

—CLAUDE HAMILTON

A TALE OF TWO SLUMPS

It was the best of times…
— CHARLES DICKENS, *A TALE OF TWO CITIES*

In the classic story *A Tale of Two Cities,* author Charles Dickens introduces us to two unforgettable characters, Charles Darnay and Sydney Carton. A powerful literary symbol in this novel is that the two cities portrayed, London and Paris, aren't as important as these two characters. The novel's real message is taught by how Sydney and Charles overcome their respective slumps and turn challenges into victories.

Therefore, a more accurate title would be: *A Tale of Two Men, Both of Whom Face Numerous High Points and Struggles in Life and Both of Whom Learn How to Overcome Slumps and Greatly Strive to Live Up to Their Potential.* Admittedly, nobody wants to read a book with that title. So an abbreviated version could simply be: *A Tale of Two Slumps.*

Few stories of climbing the Ladder from slump to success are as surprising as that of Sydney Carton. Throughout most of the book, he is in a lifelong slump, yet in the end, he overcomes it in a truly profound way. We won't spoil the story for those who haven't yet read it by giving away the plot here, but suffice it to say that even the worst slumps can be turned into great feats of heroism, service, sacrifice, and life purpose.

With this new perspective in mind — that the two "cities" in this popular classic are really Sydney and Charles instead of London and Paris — one of the most famous of Dickens's passages contains an even more powerful message. Read the following with the idea of a slump in mind:

> It was the best of times, it was the worst of times, it was the age of wisdom, it was the age of foolishness, it was the epoch of belief, it was the epoch of incredulity, it was the season of Light, it was the season of Darkness, it was the spring of hope, it was the winter of despair, we had everything before us, we had nothing before us, we were all going direct to Heaven, we were all going direct the other way…

This is an excellent description of a slump, and this quote is full of useful wisdom. In a time of slump, the person going through it almost always feels that things are bad, when in fact they are potentially "the best of times." A person in a slump thinks he or she has been foolish, or that someone else has been foolish, when the greater truth is that it is a time for an "epoch of belief." This person feels stuck in a slump of darkness when the reality is that a "season of Light" is easily within his or her reach. This person may experience a sense of despair, when he or she should feel the "spring of hope." This person wonders if all is lost, but in truth, he or she has "everything" ahead!

Another Dickens character, the infamous Scrooge in *A Christmas Carol*, also turns a life of slump into a legacy of service. The transition is hard, to be sure, and Scrooge's old habits are constant roadblocks in his needed transition to a life of higher contribution, but with enough struggle he eventually comes around.

Of course, the goal for today's leaders is to make the shift from slump to increased success much faster, more willingly, and without all the drama associated with a Dickens hero. Also, we don't want to spend our life in slumps only to rise and do something great in one grand gesture — like Sydney Carton or Scrooge. Leaders need the skill of consistently over the years turning any slump at any point in life into a win.

> **The goal for today's leaders is to make the shift from slump to increased success much faster, more willingly, and without all the drama associated with a Dickens hero.**

A second kind of slump is portrayed by Jane Austen's popular character Mr. Darcy from *Pride and Prejudice*. The book provides important lessons. For example, after Mr. Darcy tries to move on with his life following a "breakup" of epic proportions with the love of his life, Elizabeth Bennett, he finds that all the little things in life have lost their spark. He struggles with work, with social gatherings and relationships, with personal time, and in every other facet of his life. Without Lizzie, as he calls her, in his life, his joy is gone, and his focus is lost.

He wants her back, but he doesn't know how to get her. As a result, he goes into a deep funk. Everything that once felt important now loses its luster, and he ambles from activity to appointment to errand feeling lost, frustrated, and overwhelmed. His once bright future now feels empty to him, and his dreams seem irreparably dashed.

Though it doesn't say so in the novel, Darcy obviously knows that he has the power to take action, to go after what he wants, to repair earlier damages, set goals, and do whatever is needed to work toward them. But he does none of these things. He simply suffers, waiting, wishing, blaming, moping, and not daring to actually hope. In short, he does nothing. As most people often do in life, he lets the slump take over.

Clearly, both Dickens and Austen knew something about slumps. In fact, there are two major kinds of slumps that tempt people from all walks of life: the Long Slump and the Deep Slump. Almost everyone

> **We don't have to give in to any type of slump!**

experiences both at one point or another. But we don't have to give in to either type of slump. In fact, the point of this book is to teach you how to turn *any* slump into increased success — because many people don't know what is needed when a slump arises.

Tale #1: The Long Slump

This brings us to a modern tale of two slumps, the stories of Carl and Trent. The names have been changed, but both stories are true.

When Carl was in high school, he dreamed of doing something really important with his life. Mainly, he wanted to travel, see the world, and experience things beyond the cloister of his little town, the trailer park where he grew up, and even the United States. He yearned to travel the world and to make a difference in it.

Carl's father was unemployed, after being laid off from the local paper factory twelve years earlier. Carl couldn't remember a time when his dad got up in the morning and went to work. Instead, the only pattern he knew was to leave for school early, while his dad was still fast asleep, and to return home after school to do his homework while his father watched television in the other room.

Many nights, Carl struggled to sleep because the blare from his father's TV lasted well into the early hours of the morning. Carl's mother occasionally worked odd jobs in town but more often spent most of the day at her sister's home. Carl fixed most of his own meals, cleaned the house when it was needed, or left it cluttered, and tried not to make his mother or father angry.

As the years passed and he realized he had a real affinity for his studies, his dream of growing up and leaving his trailer and town forever became more and more of a possibility. He never told his parents what he planned, but when he received a full-ride scholarship to a prestigious California university, he let them know he would be leaving in a few months.

Carl worked his way through college, got excellent grades, and managed to spend two summers interning in Germany and traveling around Europe by train on weekends. His dream of seeing the world began to materialize. During his senior year, he was accepted to a graduate school in England, where he spent two additional years studying.

After working hard to complete his business training, Carl was hired as an import/export expert and traveled around the world from his company's home base in Boston. Over the years, this career fulfilled his goals of visiting many parts of the world and making a positive difference in the process. He loved his work, and he got married and had two children.

He loved that he could provide for his kids many of the things he had wished for during his childhood, not the least of which was a close parent-child relationship and a loving, happy home environment. For over two decades, Carl worked hard, served in his local church and community, and lived a busy, productive, and happy life.

Then, when Carl was in his late forties, things began to change. There was no disaster or any single moment where his life suddenly became negative, but over time, he started noticing that he just wasn't as happy as he used to be. His work brought increasing financial rewards but less personal fulfillment, and he realized that he really had no sense of important purpose. Sometimes he went for months at a time almost on autopilot, doing what needed to be done but not really living or enjoying life.

He ate poorly, rarely exercised, put on some extra weight, and found himself coming home each night after work with little energy for spending time with the family or participating in church or fun activities. He generally lost interest in the things that used to motivate him. Carl didn't volunteer for any more trips abroad, and when he was assigned to travel, he tried to get someone else to take his place.

With both of his kids now grown and living elsewhere, Carl found little joy in life. He watched more television, seldom read or listened to educational audios like he used to, and on most days, he could hardly wait for the workday to end. Then, at home on his couch, he could hardly wait for the evening to pass so he could go to bed.

Carl was in a slump, though he didn't realize it. He knew his life was dull in many ways, but he never took the chance to do anything about it or to even sit back, take stock, and call it for what it was: a desperate need to change.

The Long Slump: a gradual descent into a life slump and a slumped life.

What Carl experienced is the Long Slump: a gradual descent into a life slump and a slumped life. This coincided with a loss of purpose and passion in life.

Tale #2: The Deep Slump

The other major kind of slump is what might be called the Deep Slump. This occurs when an otherwise motivated and active person runs into a period of feeling overwhelmed, worn out, inadequate in the face of a major challenge, frustrated, unable to succeed, or just downright tired.

When you are on a path of success and leadership but run into a roadblock, distraction, crisis, or frustration that tempts you to quit, give up, or sit down and feel sorry for yourself, you are experiencing a Deep Slump. For example, Trent was so excited when his brother-in-law introduced him to a new sales business opportunity. Trent had done sales before, and he knew it could be challenging, but he had also learned that he was good at it when he just kept going to the next house and sharing his message.

He attended a couple of business meetings with his sister and her husband, listened to half a dozen audios they gave him by people who were already successful in

> **When you are on a path of success and leadership but run into a roadblock, distraction, crisis, or frustration that tempts you to quit, give up, or sit down and feel sorry for yourself, you are experiencing a Deep Slump.**

the business, and he began to dream about quitting his annoying job working for a landscaper. Trent loved what he heard on the audios. He shared many of the speakers' stories with his friends, coworkers, parents, and anyone who would listen.

Despite various negative comments from friends and family about how difficult it is to succeed in sales and/ or to start a business instead of getting a "real job" and his boss telling him to "get real," his enthusiasm increased as he continued to talk about business with his brother-in-law, attend business meetings, and listen to audios. He knew he could make this work, and he couldn't wait to get started.

Soon Trent carved out the needed time from his evenings, cut down his social and entertainment schedule, and made a list of people to call. At first, things went great. Twelve of the thirty-two people on his list of potential contacts agreed to meet with him, and eight of them actually followed through with the scheduled meeting. He met three more later that month, and two of those who initially declined to meet reconsidered when he called them back and made a personal, heartfelt plea.

All in all, he felt great about his first month in business for himself. He had met with fourteen people in four weeks, including one who just happened to be visiting a friend's house when Trent arrived there for a scheduled meeting. And he helped six people get officially started in the business. He was thrilled.

By the next month, he had exhausted his "easy list" of friends, so he brainstormed people he knew who would be amazing if only they saw the potential of the business. He called them all — former mentors, coaches, business executives, and even town leaders he had met in various capacities over the years. Five met with him, and one bought in.

This wasn't as exciting as the first month, at least not according to the numbers, but Trent had high hopes for Conrad, a manufacturing executive (and his former baseball coach) who decided to participate. Conrad told Trent that he wanted to do things in "a big way," and he held a community meeting and invited over sixty people. He advertised in the newspaper and via local radio, and the night of the event, more than a hundred people showed up.

Trent was ecstatic. When Conrad invited everyone to participate in the business, over thirty people did. Trent knew he had finally made it. He was now a bona fide leader! He was so excited to finally be living his dreams. As he drove home that evening, he mentally calculated how many people would be participating with him (at this rate of growth) in a month, six months, and a year from now. He was so energized that he couldn't fall asleep for hours.

The next month, Trent ran into a series of setbacks. He couldn't think of new people to add to his contact list, so he called all the new business members and offered to help with theirs. One by one, they made excuses, declined his help, or explained why they had decided to quit. He became frustrated and then a little upset. He wondered what he was doing wrong, but he kept trying.

Sixty days later, Trent had only eight people still participating in his business, and only two of them were actively working on the project. Despite Trent's high hopes, Conrad had stopped doing anything and was busy participating in a state-level political campaign that he supported. He told Trent that the business just wasn't very exciting to him anymore. Trent had only been able to schedule two sales meetings in the past three weeks, and the first person canceled via text message prior to the meeting.

When he showed up for the second meeting, the house was dark, and nobody answered the door. Trent walked back to his car, sat in the early winter darkness, and stared out at the snow. He shook his head, sighed, and wondered what to do.

"Is my uncle right?" he asked himself. "Is this just not a good use of my time?"

Trent sat in silence for a long time. "Should I give up? Am I just not up to this? Should I...?" His mind wandered, and he put his head in his hands and rested on the steering wheel. Eventually he turned on the car and drove home.

Three days later when Pete, one of the two friends who were still doing the business with him, called and asked for help with a new contact, Trent told him he was feeling sick and couldn't attend. He pulled a six-pack of Dr. Pepper out of the fridge and drank it while watching YouTube videos on shark attacks. This led him to more videos on bear attacks, and eventually he watched every tsunami video he could find.

When he realized it was after three o'clock in the morning, he closed his computer, stumbled to bed, and crashed for the night. Pete called the next morning, excited that he had made sales to two people the night before, but Trent was too tired to answer his phone.

Two more days went by before he pulled himself together after work and decided to address the situation. He opened his laptop, typed "Business Plan" at the top of a new document, and wondered what he should do. After a while, he went to his car and drove to the park. As he watched the beautiful snow lightly fall, he opened his computer again and tried to figure out solutions to his challenge.

He struggled with this for a while and then closed his computer and pondered. A battle raged in his mind: Give Up versus Try Harder. After ten more minutes, he'd made his decision. "I'm not giving up," he said firmly. "I'm going to make this work."

Then he tried to brainstorm. "What can I do to get out of this rut?" he wondered aloud. After fifteen minutes, he still had no ideas. He shut the computer in frustration. "What should I do?" He looked up in despair and sighed.

Trent didn't know it, but he was in a Deep Slump.

Two Slumps Compared

The solution to Trent's challenge was simple: he needed to step up to Rung 1 of the Ladder. Unfortunately, he didn't know about this rung, or any of the rungs, for that matter. He didn't know about Deep Slumps or Long Slumps. This knowledge could have been very useful.

The Long Slump is characterized by a gradual decline into mediocrity and a loss of passion for life and purpose, while the Deep Slump usually happens quickly and causes you to question your immediate and intermediate-term dreams, goals, and plans. The Long Slump is usually shallow, but it is difficult to overcome because it is based on long-held habits of mediocrity.

In contrast, the Deep Slump has more recent roots, but it usually feels deep, threatening, and insurmountable. The key word in the last sentence is "feels" because, in truth, a Deep Slump isn't really unbeatable at all; it just tends to feel that way.

> **Deep Slumps and Long Slumps are both frustrating, and both typically cause people to feel anxious, inferior, overwhelmed, and sometimes angry.**

Note that the Deep Slump is often referred to as a personal crisis, or simply a crisis. When any significant crisis comes to a person, all the feelings and struggles of Deep Slumps are present. And, in fact, there are few crises as demanding as a personal slump.

Both types of slumps are frustrating, and both typically cause people to feel anxious, inferior, overwhelmed, and sometimes angry.

Whereas a Deep Slump makes you feel like you've fallen off a cliff and nothing can be fixed, a Long Slump makes you feel like it takes too much effort to change, so you think, "Why bother?" The first makes you want to scream or cry; the second tells you just to drink another six-pack and take a longer nap. Obviously, both are bad.

Two Slumps, One Solution

What neither Carl nor Trent realized was that though there are two major types of slumps, the solution to both is almost identical. The Slump-to-Success Ladder is the same, whatever kind of slump you experience. Again, the first thing to do when you realize you are in a slump is to make sure that you never, *ever* let a good slump go to waste!

> **The first thing to do when you realize you are in a slump is to make sure that you never, *ever* let a good slump go to waste!**

WORD OF THE DAY

climb: "ascend..., scale, scramble up, clamber up, shin up..., conquer, gain..., rise..., advance..., progress, work your way..."

OPPOSITES: "descend, drop, fall."

(Compact Oxford Thesaurus)

NEVER LET A GOOD SLUMP GO TO WASTE

When P. T. Barnum of the Barnum and Bailey Circuses fame said in 1869 that, "Every cloud has a silver lining," he was paraphrasing John Milton, but he was also speaking for a generation that believed bad things could be turned into good. In the post–Civil War era of 1869, the nation desperately needed more positives.

Indeed, Barnum didn't just give lip service to silver linings; he set out to spread cheer around the country. In the midst of financial ruin from career mistakes when he was young, he planned to make a real difference in the world and ended up becoming a household name across America.

In addition to the famous circuses he established, he was also instrumental in starting Bridgeport Hospital, in improving city water systems as the mayor of Bridgeport, and in vocally speaking out on moral topics around the nation.

In truth, the Civil War itself, as much pain and suffering as it caused, accomplished much more than a silver lining. It ended slavery as an institution in the United States, and this was a great victory for freedom and morality.

> **Every great challenge has its silver linings, and every crisis is laced with major opportunities for positive, powerful change.**

Likewise, every great challenge has its silver linings, and every crisis is laced with major opportunities for positive, powerful change. The people who see past each crisis directly to the opportunities are leaders, and great leaders know that when a slump comes, the key is to look around, take stock, identify the important changes that are needed, and focus on making them.

> **The people who see past each crisis directly to the opportunities are leaders.**

As previously mentioned, while most people ("the 95 percent") see only a slump, real leaders ("the 5 percent") see only opportunities. As the old proverb puts it, when you fall down, don't forget to pick something up.

All of this is more than mottos, slogans, and maxims. It is real. Proverbs are simply the way humanity tries to pass on truly important wisdom. Again, the principles of success aren't hidden; they're just ignored by most people.

Leaders do the opposite: they embrace, apply, practice, and eventually learn to master the small and simple principles of success.

> **Great leaders know that when a slump comes, the key is to look around, take stock, identify the important changes that are needed, and focus on making them.**

The Pattern of Success

Look through the pages of history with the following question in mind: When did the great leaders emerge? The answer, spelled out in history books both ancient and modern, is very clear. The leaders emerged during crisis. This lesson is one of the main reasons most great leaders are avid readers of history. They want to learn from the past so they can be better leaders themselves. Knowing that leaders emerge during crisis is a vital piece of leadership wisdom.

For example, Noah might not even be known to history, except that his leadership in a major crisis changed the entire future. Abraham left his father and home to avoid death and ended up traveling widely and influencing the entire region. With each crisis he faced, his wisdom, leadership, and influence increased.

It is doubtful that Moses would have ever ended up in Pharaoh's court without the crisis that sent him in a baby basket out into the currents of the Nile. Another crisis led him to the desert, and then in the midst of a Long Slump, he was called to go back to Egypt and lead an entire people out of crisis. This paralleled much of the experience of his famous ancestor, Joseph.

In fact, Joseph's life provides multiple examples of both kinds of slumps. Imagine his emotions when the Deep Slump of false accusation and imprisonment turned his world upside down, not just once but twice—first when his brothers threw him into a pit and then sold him into slavery and second with Potiphar and his wife.

Imagine him languishing away for years in the Long Slump of prison and then using the crisis of Pharaoh's Deep Slump and fears about his dream to prepare the whole nation during the seven years of plenty. Joseph became a master of turning slumps into greater success.

King David's Long Slump provides many of the most touching writings known to mankind, as he recorded his feelings and lessons learned in the Psalms. The wisdom shared is profound. This pattern continues through all of Scripture.

> **With each crisis effectively overcome, wisdom, leadership, and influence increase.**

It is also a common thread in secular literature and history. In fact, Homer gave us a word for the long, difficult attempt to overcome a Long Slump. The word is "Odyssey." In the great classic by this name, Homer shows how one man, Odysseus, deals with an onslaught of life challenges and ultimately keeps his focus on what really matters most to him: getting back home to his wife and family.

Homer's earlier classic, the *Iliad*, describes how several potentially great leaders dealt with their Deep Slumps when Helen of Troy was captured and carried away by an enemy army. Some of these men rose to the level of real leadership, and others fell short. The key factor of success versus failure for these men was found in the way they applied, or failed to apply, true principles.

In a similar vein, Shakespeare wrote a major set of plays about people facing the immediate fear, struggle, and difficulty of a Deep Slump, and he wrote another entire group of plays about people dealing with and trying to overcome bigger, more lasting, Long-Slump life challenges, weaknesses, and problems. The first kind of plays is known as Comedy, and the second as Tragedy.

Actually, the use of the word *comedy* here is interesting. These plays are known as comic not because they are funny (that's not what the word *comedy* originally meant) but rather because someone in each play rises above a Deep Slump of crisis and overload and instead stays focused on the opportunity each difficulty presents. Such leaders naturally bring about positive results, after great struggle, and the plays end with most of the characters laughing, singing, and rejoicing together. This joy is the source of the word *comedy* used to describe such plays.

In contrast, however, the characters who didn't apply true principles of integrity, morality, and life success are left unhappy and unimproved. Shakespeare carefully shows us many types of characters and the results of their choices in each play. The two groups of characters choose between focusing on the opportunities or the problems and applying true principles or giving in to the worries, fears, and struggles that accompany every slump and every crisis. This profound choice, put more succinctly, boils down to the phrase: "to be or not to be…"

Before any major progress in history, there is always a period of slump and crisis and then victory and advancement. Likewise, prior to any great success by an individual or team, there is always a slump, a challenge, and a choice. The decision—whether to remain loyal to true principles or to "curse the stars" and break principles, as Romeo and Othello did—determines all outcomes.

> **Before any major progress in history, there is always a period of slump and crisis and then victory and advancement.**

Those who stick to principles and truth, who do the right thing against whatever challenges arise, emerge as leaders. They also emerge happier, more successful, and better off than before the slump and crisis ever occurred. This doesn't mean that great leaders go around hoping for slumps, but when a slump does come, they focus on the opportunities that come with it.

> **Prior to any great success by an individual or team, there is always a slump, a challenge, and a choice.**

This connection between slumps, crises, opportunities, choices, principles, and consequences runs through all history and literature. It is repeated so frequently in Scripture that it is clearly a major theme and so often in literature that it is obviously a leading human challenge.

Simple and True

Let's make this as explicit as possible. What is often lost to most people is the following simple reality: when any slump or crisis occurs, the key is to quickly look around for the wonderful opportunity that comes with every difficulty. This is a law of the universe, a principle, a fact:

When a challenge comes, an opportunity comes with it.

Great leaders, and those who want to become great leaders, learn to happily and enthusiastically greet every slump, crisis, and problem by immediately looking around for the opportunity. They know it's there because they know this is a law of truth.

Over time, great leaders learn to go a step further:

*They look for and find more than one opportunity
in every difficulty.*

Moreover, they focus on these opportunities, give them their best attention and effort, and go to work shaping and molding the opportunities to their full potential. This is both an art and a science. Leaders are scientists when they immediately, predictably, and rigorously look past any slump and seek out the opportunities it brings. And they are artists as they infuse their passion, vision, creativity, and resources to make these opportunities flourish.

In short, a slump is a terrible thing to waste. When you realize you are in a slump of any kind, immediately brainstorm and write down all the opportunities it brings. Give this real time and effort. Then go to work turning the opportunities into great successes.

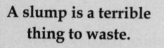

A slump is a terrible thing to waste.

This is how leaders see the world. This is what it means to have a leadership mentality. And those who do this, who turn the opportunities into real progress, naturally become great leaders.

Seven Sage Suggestions

Business leader and bestselling author Claude Hamilton teaches that when you want to pull out of a slump, there are several key attitudes and behaviors that will make a huge positive difference. These[6] include the following:

1. "Don't let a slump be contagious," either at work or in your family. If you are facing a slump, don't go around infecting other people with your struggles. Focus on the opportunities, and help other people

get excited about these instead of embroiling them in your worries or negative feelings.

2. "Get momentum" going in the right direction by finding one positive thing you can do really well and making sure you do it. Just the act of doing one thing really well will help you get other things going also. If you don't start excelling in at least one thing, your slump will linger.

3. "Act 'as if...' or 'fake it till you make it.'" This doesn't mean to act like something you're not or to try to falsely impress people. Rather, Hamilton teaches that it means to act like you *should* act, even when you feel down in a slump. Act like you should! This is powerful.

4. "Take one day at a time." Know what you should be doing today, and do it. Do it well—even when you don't quite feel like it, *especially* when you don't feel like it! Doing the right thing today is a powerful action that starts spreading anti-slump energy in your heart and mind. In contrast, failing to do the right thing today will surely make the slump worse.

5. "Be grateful for what you have." Be thankful. An attitude of gratitude will do wonders for any slump, just like an attitude of thanklessness will always add fuel to the negativity in your

life. Successful people are grateful, even for the challenges they face.

6.   "Never quit when you're down." Too often, people experiencing a slump think that everything is better than what they *should* be doing right now. Some people spend much of their lives constantly starting new things and then just giving up when they face a roadblock or slump. They seldom finish

> **Don't use a slump as an excuse to quit.**

anything. This is a guaranteed path to unhappiness, repeated failures, and an unfulfilling lifelong slump. Don't take this route. Don't use a slump as an excuse to quit.

7.   "Don't beat yourself up during a slump." Attacking yourself for your problems isn't going to help you get out of them. Focus on solutions, not on self-criticism. As business leader and *New York Times* bestselling author Orrin Woodward said, "Imagine that you were walking down the street, and some stranger came up and said the things to you that you've been saying to yourself in your head. You'd be outraged!"

In a slump, aim for solutions and focus on positive thoughts that can help you overcome your problems. As Hamilton put it: "Be careful of negative chatter in your head."

Also: "When you pull yourself up out of slump after slump after slump, when you go through rainstorm after rainstorm and the sun comes out again and again, it makes you stronger....It makes you more successful at whatever you're doing."

Real leaders know how to turn any slump into increased progress and more excellence. This is an essential skill for achieving any kind of serious success.

We all need to learn how to do this, one rung at a time. In fact, there are six rungs on the Slump-to-Success Ladder, six steps that help us climb out of any slump and turn frustration, crisis, and opportunity into increased accomplishments, successes, and victories.

> **Real leaders know how to turn any slump into increased progress and more excellence.**

The best place to start learning about the Ladder is with the first rung.

WORD OF THE DAY

step: "stair, tread; rung...; stairway, staircase..., course of action, measure, move, act..., initiative..., advance..., movement; breakthrough..., increase, intensify, strengthen, augment, escalate...; accelerate, quicken, hasten..."

(Compact Oxford Thesaurus)

When Life Gives You Lemons...

"When life gets you down, you know what
you gotta do? Just keep swimming. Just
keep swimming. Just keep swimming,
swimming, swimming..."
— Dory, *Finding Nemo*

"When you're in a Slump,
you're not in for much fun.
Un-slumping yourself
is not easily done."
— Dr. Seuss, *Oh, the Places You'll Go!*

"My motto was always to keep swinging.
Whether I was in a slump or
feeling badly or having trouble off the field,
the only thing to do was keep swinging."
— Hank Aaron

"I had slumps that lasted into the winter."
— Bob Uecker

"It is absolutely essential to hang
in there—especially when you
feel most discouraged."
—Steven R. Shallenberger

"A new challenge keeps the brain
kicking and the heart ticking."
—E. A. Bucchianeri

"When you come to the edge of
all that you know, you must believe
one of two things: either there will be
ground to stand on, or you will
be given wings to fly."
—O. R. Melling, *The Summer King*

RUNG 1:
TAKE ACTION!

The early bird gets the worm.
— CITED BY WILLIAM CAMDEN,
ENGLISH HISTORIAN, IN 1605

When you are in a slump, it often feels like every part of you resists doing anything about it. You expend a great deal of energy, but it's on complaining, moping and sighing, thinking about your plight, blaming things on other people or circumstances, asking "what if?" or "if only?" and looping your worries in your mind over and over. And behaviors like these don't fix anything.

In most cases, all this effort just makes you feel worse. This is the kind of "busy" that is worse than doing nothing because it only increases your problems and worries.

> **Waiting makes slumps even worse.**

Likewise, waiting makes slumps even worse. It is very possible to turn a Deep Slump or a Long Slump into a full-blown Life Slump (where the slump is both Deep and Long at the same time) simply by waiting around. When a slump comes, waiting is the worst-case scenario. Don't wait. Act.

> **When a slump comes, waiting is the worst-case scenario. Don't wait. Act.**

Consider the following words on this important topic from authors Chris Brady and Orrin Woodward:

There are two reactions people exhibit when confronted with challenges. The first is the most common. It involves the wearing of a long face, the art of moping, and the self-protective mechanism of retreating into one's shell. Picture a roly poly bug. At the first sign of trouble, he curls up in a ball, hoping nobody can see him and hoping beyond hope that some snot-nosed toddler doesn't pick him up, roll him around, and ultimately squish him....

[This] reaction to the problem amplifies the problem instead of erasing it. [People] become paralyzed, their activity slows down, they over-think every angle of their situation, and, in short, they haul off and do a lot of nothing.

The second reaction is the correct one. It involves the taking of massive action against the problem.

That's a great phrase: "taking...*massive action* against the problem." That's how you deal with a slump. That's the leadership spirit. That's grit. Guts. Courage. It's also wisdom. Because when you don't take action, the slump gets worse.

Brady and Woodward continue:

It is the old maxim, "It's time to do something even if it's wrong." This reaction may or may not be perfect, but because it involves action it usually leads to adjustments over time and therefore becomes more and more productive. As it has been said, a car is easier to steer once it's moving.

This is worth repeating over and over. By taking action when you find yourself in a slump, you set yourself on a path of fixing things. Of improving your situation. Of building success. Yes, you might

> **When you don't take action, the slump gets worse.**

make mistakes, but mistakes can be dealt with and adjustments can be made. In fact, the normal, natural process of taking action includes making adjustments as needed.

In contrast, the normal flow of waiting around in your slump just leads to becoming more deeply slumped, and this can last for a very long time. It is no exaggeration that most people — *most* people! — in this world spend many years in slumps. Some people spend most of their life in slumps.

That's a real definition of tragedy. Everyone faces challenges, and everyone experiences slumps, but turning a slump into increased progress is the very definition of success, while letting a slump fester and last is true tragedy. Living in a slump isn't really living.

As Brady and Woodward put it:

Action is the key. Character is exhibited by the action of the individual in the face of paralyzing pressures. When the average person would curl up like a bug, the champion comes out swinging.

That's the way out of a slump. Start swinging! Start moving. Take action. That's Rung 1 of the Slump-to-Success Ladder. Make adjustments as you go, but first you've got to get going!

> **Living in a slump isn't really living.**

As we said above, in a slump, action is usually the last thing you feel like engaging. But it's the first thing you must embrace. Without action, all is lost.

Brady and Woodward continue:

Never underestimate the power of massive action to initiate a whole train of events that can pull you out of your problem.

This is true. This is powerful. Don't sit in a slump! Get moving. You'll be amazed at the "train of events" that will follow.

Its cumulative impact is often hard to believe. Progress stacks upon progress, challenges recede [but only if you act!], breaks seem to happen in an increasingly positive direction, and the sky begins to clear.

But none of that will happen if you sit on the couch, mope, blame, or stay paralyzed by your problems. Get up and get moving. The world is passing by and takes little notice of those who play the victim. Quit losing and get moving. Action is the key.[7]

> **"Quit losing and get moving."**
> — Chris Brady and Orrin Woodward

This is incredibly wise counsel. Taking action works! It is Rung 1 of the Ladder out of a slump.

Two Examples

For example, remember the stories of Carl and Trent from earlier in the book? Both of them got caught in a slump, and both of them engaged in some negative and destructive behaviors. But by the end of the stories, one of them did the right thing, and the other stayed a prisoner to his slump. Do you remember which?

Here's a little help. Carl did the wrong thing. Here's how his story ended:

He watched more television, seldom read or listened to educational audios like he used to, and on most days, he could hardly wait for the workday to end. Then, at home on his couch, he could hardly wait for the evening to pass so he could go to bed.

Carl was in a slump, though he didn't realize it. He knew his life was dull in many ways, but he never took the chance to do anything about it or to even sit back, take stock, and call it for what it was: a desperate need to change.

By not taking action, Carl was never able to get past his slump. His Long Slump tragically turned into a Life Slump. He can still turn it around, certainly, but so far he hasn't. He still drinks himself to sleep each night in front of an endless parade of trivial television shows that are mostly forgotten a day later. His talents are shared a bit each day at work but are mostly going to waste in a world that desperately needs the gifts, knowledge, and skills he once worked so hard to obtain.

The passion Carl showed as a young man, fighting to get out the trailer park and into the best schools, to travel the world, to get a prestigious education, and to make a difference, are all past. Now he…sits. A lot. Slumps are that way. They can turn great potential into puddles of carbon and water sitting on couches for endless, mediocre hours.

In contrast, Trent took a different path. He made one little choice that changed everything. Yes, he moped and whined for a few days, but then one evening after work, he did something different. It seemed like a small thing at the time, but it was actually huge, though he didn't realize it until years later.

Here's what happened:

Two more days went by before he pulled himself together after work and decided to address the situation. He opened his laptop, typed "Business Plan" at the top of a new document, and wondered what he should do. After a while, he went to his car and drove to the park. As he watched the beautiful snow lightly fall, he opened his computer again and tried to figure out solutions to his challenge....

Then he tried to brainstorm. "What can I do to get out of this rut?" he wondered aloud. After fifteen minutes, he still had no ideas. He shut the computer in frustration. "What should I do?" He looked up in despair and sighed.

Trent was in a bad place, but he was also in the *right* place — trying to make a plan, brainstorming ideas, taking action. Because he left the couch and acted, the next step was natural: deeply frustrated, he called his mentor, his brother-in-law, and told him about his struggle.

After he completely unburdened his worries, setbacks, and feelings of inadequacy to his mentor, he finally ran out of things to say. Then his mentor told him something powerful, something that he had heard before. Fortunately, he was now ready to really listen.

"Trent, let's get Pete, Jennifer, and a few of my other team members together and work on this as a group," he heard his mentor say. "There are a number of tools we can use. We just have to meet and decide what to do first."

Something immediately switched in Trent's gut. It was like a light bulb turning on, and the gloomy feeling of the past several weeks started to dissipate. Trent sat up straight in his seat, and for the first time in days, he realized he was smiling. "That sounds great. When can we meet? I'll call Pete and Jennifer right now and then Heather!"

Action leads to action, just like inaction causes more inaction. Rung 1 of the Slump-to-Success Ladder is to take action, *"massive action,"* as Brady and Woodward put it. When you do this, any slump in your life is suddenly an endangered species. Besides, from the higher vantage point provided by stepping up to the first rung of action, everything looks brighter and better.

Today Trent is building a successful business, to the point that he has been able to "retire" from his day job and now works on his business full-time. Each year his success increases, and he has earned the respect and admiration of his uncle, his friends, and the various naysayers who once tried to talk him out of going into business for himself.

Once in a while, Trent gets a call from someone in his business who needs help and says, "Things just aren't working....What should I do?"

On numerous occasions, Trent has helped the person calm down and told him or her a powerful story: "I still remember the day I decided not to give up no matter what. I was sitting in my car with my laptop open, trying to brainstorm solutions to my business problems. The snow was coming down, and I felt so scared, so little, so inadequate.

"Then after a while, I closed my computer and looked out my car windows. I knew I had a choice to make. I could quit. It would be easy. What could be easier? But as soon as this thought came to me, something else happened. A feeling rose inside me, and I knew. I knew I wouldn't quit.

> **Simply refuse to give up!**

"Actually, I *decided* it. I *chose* it. I simply refused to give up. I had no idea what I was going to do, but I knew I was going to keep trying. As soon as I made that decision, I opened my computer again, and I immediately thought to call my mentor. The rest is history...."

Take action. When your darkest day comes, take action. When the big challenge comes into your life, take action. When you are at your lowest, take action. When your Goliath, your desert experience, your Valley Forge comes, take action. In fact, don't wait for any of these things to spur you to action. When the very hint of a slump, a challenge, a setback, or a negative appears in your

> **When your darkest day comes, take action.**

> **When your Goliath, your desert experience, your Valley Forge comes, take action.**

life, look around immediately. If you look, you'll find an opportunity, and when you do, take action.

WORD OF THE DAY

reliable: "trustworthy, dependable, good, true, faithful, devoted, steadfast, staunch, constant, loyal, trusty, dedicated, unfailing..."

OPPOSITE: "untrustworthy"

(Compact Oxford Thesaurus)

RUNG 2: PLAN A TWO-DAY VACATION

Stop worrying and start living.
—DALE CARNEGIE

If you're in a slump, getting out of it is imperative to your success. And the first action to get you out of a slump is to go on vacation.

That's right. Vacation.

This might seem counter-intuitive, surprising, or even downright wrong. But when you find yourself in a slump, the key is to take action, and few actions are as effective as the right kind of vacation.

> **When you find yourself in a slump, the key is to take action, and few actions are as effective as the right kind of vacation.**

In fact, a vacation is the perfect anti-slump action because it breaks the negative pattern—quickly. Here's how it works: you go straight from the thought "I'm in a slump, darn it" to "this is a great opportunity; I need to take action right away. The first thing I'm going to do is take a two-day vacation! Perfect!"

Mind you, we're not talking about a weeklong vacation; that gives you too much time to loop worries over and over in your mind. An afternoon escape won't work either, though; that makes it too easy to mope and complain and return unchanged to the same old routine. No, a two-day vacation is just right.

You can drive to your brother's house two hours away, or check in to a lodge in the mountains. Or if you prefer, you can book a hotel in your own city — on the other side of town. Make arrangements for things to be taken care of at home, and pack light. If you can't get off work, go on the weekend.

Regardless, find a way to take a vacation and break the pattern. Put yourself in a new place doing something different for a couple of days. That's the first part of Rung 2.

The second part is even simpler: throw a large pile of positive audios into your car or bag, and take them with you. Choose audios from people who have proven success, people who can help you switch your negative inner self-talk to positive. And most important of all, *listen* to the audios.

One thing is absolutely certain. If you're in a slump, many of your thoughts are negative, and negative thinking naturally brings negative results. If you're caught in nega-tive mental behaviors, your slump isn't going to turn around. So pick out a bunch of positive audios and take them with you on your two-day mini getaway.

The third part of your vacation is to set a deadline for when your slump will be over, preferably the instant you return home from your two-day vacation. This is *very* important. Write this down:

> *The second I get home from this vacation, my slump will be entirely over. Period.*

Negative thinking naturally brings negative results. If you're caught in negative mental behaviors, your slump isn't going to turn around. So pick out a bunch of positive audios and take them with you on your two-day mini getaway.

Write it on a sticky note and post it on your dashboard, or make it your phone's background so you see it every time you glance at the screen. Or put it on the calendar on your desk. Find a place that works for you, and read this message several times a day.

The fourth part is the most fun: Go on your vacation. And listen to the audios the whole time you're traveling. Use headphones if you're going to be in public. But listen, listen, listen.

Just listen.

This isn't any old vacation, after all. It's an anti-slump vacation. And you're going to fill it with positive voices sharing positive messages and examples of success.

Of course, it could be argued that, at times, some people take the concept of positivity a little far. But when you're in a slump, that's the furthest thing from your problem. You need as much positivity as possible. You need to douse your thinking in positive ideas and feelings and then immerse it in more of the same.

You need to jump into a lake of positive thinking, shared by people who have proven success in life, and then swim around until you're all wet with positive feelings and thoughts. You need to wash away the grime of stinkin' thinking.

That's what your vacation is for.

This is powerful action because it works. When you listen to hours of positive, uplifting, realistic, proven, quality ideas and messages from excellent, effective leaders, your mental state goes through a quiet but predictable shift. The positive receptors in your brain boot up, so to speak, and the negative neural pathways stop ruining your thoughts and feelings.

> **When you listen to hours of positive, uplifting, realistic, proven, quality ideas and messages from excellent, effective leaders, your mental state goes through a quiet but predictable shift.**

There are more details to the actual science of such changes,[8] to be sure, but the main thing is that a vacation steeped in real learning and personal improvement gets you ready for the next rung. It's hard to climb the rungs to effective action when you're caught in a sea of negativity.

Yes, this can be overstated in many situations. The movies poke fun at people who think a "Silver Lining" approach to life is all you need. It's not. But it certainly is an important part of progress and success. And when you find yourself in a slump, positive feelings can be a huge help. They are, in fact, *necessary*.

> **When you find yourself in a slump, positive feelings can be a huge help. They are, in fact, *necessary*.**

You'll need more than this, of course. That's what the other rungs are about. But this is part of getting out of any slump. Watch anyone who is in a slump, and you'll see that unless a real increase in positive input is part of that person's daily life, he or she will stay stuck.

Your thoughts matter. If they're negative, you're going to go in the wrong direction. Get them going on the positive path. As Chris Brady and Orrin Woodward wrote: "Your dream cannot be stolen, but through poor thinking, it can be surrendered."[9] Immerse your thoughts in positives.

Go on a vacation, do some fun things, get some rest if possible, catch some rays or swim, surf, or watch the river, but make sure you soak up a ton of positive, important ideas and feelings. Without a boost in positive words and thoughts, you'll stay in a rut.

This is all very simple—so simple, in fact, that most people shake it off as a bit juvenile. But great leaders know that when they're in a slump, they need a brief change of scenery and a healthy increased dose of positive voices. That's the 5 percent approach. As Chris Brady put it: "This time away is meant to be used to refresh your dream and get back to the 'Why' instead of drowning in the 'Now.'"

It's amazing what just two days and a night to sleep on things can do for any slump. The restorative power of such a mini vacation is hard to overstate.

If you tend to be a workaholic and vacations are frustrating to you, use the time to write down a long list of lessons and ideas you learn from the audios. Catalog them, and share them with someone when you get home. This will give your "I have to be busy" personality an outlet, and at the same time, it will increase what you learn and retain.

But remember that the goal isn't so much to remember the things you learn from the audios; it's to *feel* and *think* differently, more positively, more creatively, for a couple of days. That's what makes this a vacation. You're not going to get answers to your problems; you're on vacation to break the daily routine of your slump and to infuse your mind and emotions with positive feelings, stories, and ideas.

Some people prefer reading to listening, so do what works best for you. For many people, both listening to audios and reading are extremely helpful. Read and listen to uplifting, powerful teachings from people who have succeeded and know the right words, principles, and lessons to share.

Such teachings, whether written or spoken, allow you to relax, kick back a little, and let your brain dwell on positive thoughts shared by others. Without such positives, people too often allow negative thoughts to rule the day.

Such negative drift is much less likely when you are listening to the right kind of audios and reading the right kind of books. Even if your brain starts looping back to your rut, your ears and eyes will be taking in the positives. The ensuing battle is good for you because it will bring more positive feelings.

While you are listening to the audios and reading, your negative thoughts and emotions will go on vacation for a few hours. And several such blocks of positive influx over the two-day period will break up your slump pattern. That's really what this whole mini vacation is all about; it's not so much a vacation from work as a vacation for your mind from the slump.

This works. It is especially effective when you've established a deadline for the slump. You know the slump will be over the moment you return home, so you can focus on enjoying the vacation. The more fun you have, the better. Any time negatives pop up, turn your audios back on and let them do battle against the negative neural pathways and bad thinking habits.

> **Any time negatives pop up, turn your audios back on and let them do battle against the negative neural pathways and bad thinking habits.**

For example, this is a representation of your brain on continual negatives (negative, negative, negative, negative…):

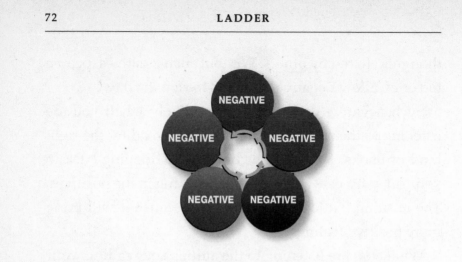

In contrast, this is your brain on the right kind of ideas, stories, thoughts, and feelings:

It's positive, positive, positive, positive…and upward.

While negative thoughts and feelings loop in a cycle that repeats itself and creates slumps, the positive pattern is different. Positive thoughts, words, ideas, and feelings spark other positives in an upward push toward creativity, innovation, advancement, solutions, and improvements.

This list of positive synonyms is worth reading and rereading:

Success	Achievement	Thrive
Progress	Accomplishment	Blossom
Advancement	Victory	Bloom
Creativity	Triumph	Increase
Innovation	Realization	Overcome
Solution	Attainment	Adapt
Initiative	Prosperity	Lead
Ingenuity	Flourish	Improve
Prevailingness	Development	Grow
Win	Rally	Imagine
Wisdom	Skill	Invent
Fulfillment	Execution	Bear Fruit
Knowledge	Proficiency	Shine

There are many more words that could be added. Just reading this list is a powerful exercise for a person in a slump, as it activates a part of the mind that frequently brings a smile and a spark of initiative. This is powerful because action breeds action.

Indeed, the negative loop

can't compete very well with the catalyst of positive originality, vision, and inspiration that always accompanies genuine leadership energy:

The difference is significant. Light eventually wins out against darkness. Truth always ultimately trumps falsehoods. When you give positives a real chance, the negatives dissipate, and light wins. It really is "the best of times," not "the worst..."

Again, too many people dismiss this because it seems too simple and too easy. But anyone who has worked on mastering his or her thoughts and feelings knows that this

> **When you give positives a real chance, the negatives dissipate, and light wins.**

skill is actually incredibly difficult. Few people are able to do it well, and even fewer keep doing it over time.

Thought mastery is amazingly rare. Choosing positives over negatives, even when difficult challenges arise in life, is hard. Those who learn how to do it, and do it consistently, are always going to experience much more success than those who don't. It's one of the most challenging things a person can do. In the words of business leader Dan Hawkins, "Belief is the hardest work you will do."[10]

Yet it is made much easier if we simply listen to audios and read books from people who have learned to do this consistently, even routinely. The thought patterns, word patterns, and even the quotes, stories, and ideas shared by people who have paid the price to gain the powerful level of thought mastery necessary for great successes in life have a real, effective impact on our own efforts to emphasize the positive.

Those who immerse themselves in such beneficial teachings invite the powerful forces of creativity, innovative thinking, and anti-slump enthusiasm into their lives. This is significant.

When a slump comes, immediately start looking for the opportunities in it. Take action right away by going on a two-day vacation, with a preset deadline for your slump to end the instant you return home. And listen to positive audios and read great books to fill your mind with the right kind of thoughts and create an environment to really turn a slump into a bigger success.

Then, when you get home, your slump is over. You'll arrive back home in a different place because the negative patterns of a slump will be greatly weakened, and your internal leader will be feeling a sense of possibility and excitement.

You'll still have some very important decisions to make and some hard work ahead to really get over any serious slump. Feeling positive for two days isn't going to magically make everything easy or scare all your problems away. But unless you engage the positive, nothing is going to fix your slump.

Without switching on some positivity in your life, your slump is going to hang around a lot longer. When you bring in the positive, even just a little, you take a step up to a higher rung of the Slump-to-Success Ladder. That little step will make a huge difference.

> **When you bring in the positive, even just a little, you take a step up to a higher rung of the Slump-to-Success Ladder.**

Again, there's more to do, no doubt about it. But when you take this step, you'll be genuinely ready to take the next one as well.

WORD OF THE DAY

remarkable: "extraordinary, exceptional, amazing, astonishing, astounding, marvelous, wonderful, sensational, stunning, incredible..."

OPPOSITE: "ordinary"

(Compact Oxford Thesaurus)

There is a world of difference
between knowing what to do
and actually doing it.
—BILL PHILLIPS

RUNG 3:
RELEASE THE POWER

Seek and you will find…
—MATTHEW 7:7

But wait! There's one more thing you need to do before you drive or fly away on your vacation. It won't take long, but it's very important.

Before you even leave your house on your vacation, you need to remember a few key steps to the next rung, which will subconsciously work on you during your entire two-day vacation and add a further dimension to your focus on positivity. Chris Brady calls this process focusing on your "Dreams, Cause, Calling, and Legacy." Here are the steps of this rung in a simple four-part overview:

1. **Remember Your Dream!** Ask yourself, "What is my Dream?" If you already know the answer to this question, write it down and move on to the next step. If you're not sure what your biggest Dreams are, brainstorm some, making sure to be

open and creative. It's essential to actually write down your Dreams. Put them on paper; don't just keep them in your mind. Doing so makes the Dreams concrete, real, physical.

Once you have some Dreams written, narrow them down to those that really matter to you. This is a crucial step because it puts everything in perspective and helps you reframe your slump in the context of what you really care about. Skipping this short step is a mistake because it is almost impossible for a slump to last when it is held up to the light of your powerful Dreams. As with so many other basics in this book, this is so simple that many people just ignore it. But leaders know better. They know that the basics are the key to all success. Do the basics.

Finally, take the paper with your Dreams written on it with you on your vacation and read over them several times a day. This will help your mind focus on what's

> **The basics are the key to all success.**

really important, and that's powerful anti-slump medicine. If you can't leave on your vacation for several days, read the paper every day between now and when you get home from the vacation. Trust us. What you put into your mind has immense influence. Garbage in, garbage out. Or more important, your Dreams in, your Dreams out!

2. **What Is Your Cause?** Follow this same process in determining or remembering and writing down your Cause. What do you really want to support, help, and change in the world? If you don't know, brainstorm. As soon as you do know your Cause, write it down. This is a powerful and effective exercise for anyone in a slump. Just remembering your Cause is extremely helpful. Write it, take it with you on your vacation, and read it multiple times a day, along with your Dreams, on the same days that you are reading great things and listening to several blocks of positive audios.

3. **What Is Your Calling?** Now, do the same thing with your Calling. What are you called to do in life? If you know, write it down. If not, brainstorm, and write what you feel. Write it, and read it often.

4. **What Is Your Legacy?** Finally, take these same steps to determine your Legacy. How do you want to be remembered? Write this down, and read it often.

These steps are very beneficial. The combination of your Dreams, Cause, Calling, and Legacy is incredibly powerful. Together, these are called your "Dreams and Motivations." Just remembering them deals a strong blow to any slump. It's almost impossible not to start taking the actions that will get you out of a slump if you complete these beneficial steps and read your Dreams and Motivations several times a day for two days or more.

People who write down their Dreams, Cause, Calling, and Legacy and read them at least three times a day are usually back on track for real success within just a few days. In fact, the Dreams and Motivations are so powerful that people who really don't want to get out of a slump — for whatever reason — almost always refuse to write these things down, much less read them several times daily.

Don't let the simplicity of this little exercise fool you. It may speak softly, but the Dreams and Motivations truly do carry a big stick. They work. Anyone can do this easy yet powerful exercise, and those who do almost always see rapid, major results. They may not always see everything fixed overnight because there are Ladder rungs that need to be climbed, but the results do happen. The Dreams and Motivations exercise works so well, in fact, that you'll want to keep doing it the day after your vacation, the day after that, and every day for weeks and even months to follow. The results are truly amazing, not only in a slump but every day of your life.

Track your use of the Dreams and Motivations tool, and you'll find that slumps almost never occur when you're reading your Dreams and Motivations frequently each day. Our Dreams, Cause, Calling, and Legacy keep us on target, increase our focus, and keep us consciously thinking about what's really important. This is the best way to hurdle slumps: simply avoid them and keep progressing forward by staying focused on what really matters to you.

Update your Dreams and Motivations as needed. (Most people find that they need to do this at least every six months or so.) Post copies on your bathroom mirror, your desk, your laptop, your briefcase, your dashboard—anywhere you'll remember to read them daily. Keep them short and focused so you can read them in less than a minute or two. And to help you take action on your Dreams and Motivations, create and regularly update a written Game Plan with one-year, five-year, and long-term goals and daily and weekly To-Do Lists for achieving those goals.

Seeing the success that comes from a continual focus on one's Dreams and Motivations is an excellent example of when the 95 percent tend to think that the 5 percent have some special secret of success, know someone in high places, or just have more luck than everyone else. However, the fact remains that great leaders simply do the basics more consistently than other people.

> **Great leaders simply do the basics more consistently than other people.**

If you don't read your Dreams, Cause, Calling, and Legacy several times a day, your days will be spent focused on something else. Result? Years from now, you'll have achieved something else instead of your real goals. The leaders who seem lucky are where they are because they stayed focused on their Dreams and Motivations and didn't let anything else get in the way of achieving them. How could they? After all, it's hard to get distracted when you're reading your Dreams and Motivations in the morning, at breakfast, during lunch, at dinner, and prior to going to bed.

Success isn't a secret. It's the result of small and simple things, the little things that generate consistent momentum, focus, and power. Books like this one are emphatically trying to convince more and more people to do the little habits that make all the difference and bring big results. Of these, few are more powerful than the Dreams and Motivations exercise. With consistent use, you'll see your productivity, positivity, and eventually profitability increase.

> **Success isn't a secret. It's the result of small and simple things, the little things that generate consistent momentum, focus, and power.**

Go Have Fun

As for the vacation, go have fun. If you're not sure where to go or what to do, search online for "best mini vacation" along with the name of your state, province, or area. You can also try variations like "best budget vacation" or "best day trip" combined with the name of your region. You'll get a whole list of options.

> **Some of the best vacations cost very little and consist mostly of lounging around listening to the right audios and reading the right books.**

A quick vacation is a very important rung on the Slump-to-Success Ladder. Don't skip it. Some of the best vacations cost very little and consist mostly of lounging around listening to the right audios and reading the right books. But get away from your regular home and office and spend your time somewhere else.

This can be as simple as getting up in the morning and driving to spend the whole day at a Barnes and Noble, reading books, listening to audios, and reviewing your Dreams and Motivations, and then doing the same thing the next day. A library or park can be just as good. The key is to stay there all day, for two full days.

Recharge. Refill the positive. Refocus on what you really care about. Relax and decompress.

And have as much fun as you can.

WORD OF THE DAY

key: "crucial, central, essential, pivotal, critical..., vital, principal, prime, chief, major, leading, main, important, significant."

OPPOSITE: "peripheral"

(Compact Oxford Thesaurus)

RUNG 4: LET YOUR SLUMP ROLL...

Much ado about nothing...
—WILLIAM SHAKESPEARE, 1598

Take your two-day vacation, and let your slump roll! Make your mini vacation a great slump! Don't work— just slump. Vacation. Relax. Smile. Laugh. Read books and listen to positive audios from proven leaders. Read your Dreams and Motivations when you wake up, just before you go to bed, and at every meal.

Get some fresh air, or visit an interesting place. Tour a museum, attend a play, throw a Frisbee with your friend or your dog. Get some sun, swim, or walk on the beach. Ski, or read. Do whatever you most love to do on vacation. Spend time with loved ones.

Or just find a comfortable chair and relax. Watch the sunrise and keep watching until after sunset. Smell the flowers. Dream of world peace. Cross the road...just to get to the other side. Chase a rainbow.

All joking aside, take a fun two-day vacation. Whatever you choose to do during this time, drink lots of water, read great books, and listen to so many positive audios that you wear out a pair of ear buds.

A vacation is a great way to decompress and reboot.

Experiences in Mini Vacations

Books and movies portray a number of people following this pattern of using a quick getaway to reboot and rejuvenate during a slump. For example, even wizards like Gandalf in *The Lord of the Rings* trilogy sometimes take a break from their serious, challenging lives to vacation in the Shire and watch some fireworks.

In Austen's *Pride and Prejudice*, no matter how bad things get, Elizabeth Bennett deals with them effectively by taking long walks. When things are especially difficult, a mini vacation with her aunt and uncle helps turn everything around.

Ebenezer Scrooge makes huge changes in just one night that is clearly outside of his normal experience. Imagine what he might have accomplished if he'd kept at it for another night as well!

> *"Bueller, Bueller, Bueller..."*
> — Economics Teacher,
> *Ferris Bueller's Day Off*

Or consider the popular movie *Ferris Bueller's Day Off*. In this comedic spoof on the whole genre of Eighties high school movies, young Ferris Bueller finds his life caught in a real high school slump. Just

listening to one of his teachers call the class roll in mono-
tone — "Bueller, Bueller, Bueller..." — is enough to remind
most adults of similar high school ruts.

In a packed one-day vacation from his regular life,
Ferris does everything differently. He gets in trouble,
helps his best friend Cameron get in trouble as well, and
generally gets away from his normal routine in a search to
overcome his slump and recharge his life. In the process,
he learns about treating people better, has experiences he
never dreamed of, and faces some real challenges.

By the time the day off is over, it's clear that Ferris
Bueller's regular life isn't so bad after all. This one day
away from the norm prepares him to return to school more
positive, less slumped, better connected with his family
members and values, and more ready to engage with life.

It also helps Cameron, who is in an even worse slump,
to improve and refocus. That's what a good mini vacation
does. Just imagine how exciting things could have gotten
for Ferris if he'd taken a second day off as well.

A two-day vacation from your slump/rut/crisis almost
always provides enough change for you to take the initiative and guide your life in a different direction. It's like
a spark, or a lift-off, to the changes you need. There are
many other examples. In Owen Wister's classic book
The Virginian, the hardworking, no-nonsense Wyoming
cowboy and hero of the story is nearly always engaged in
his important job. But once in a while, especially during
a slump, he goes to the well, pulls up a bucket of water,

washes his face and hair, puts on his best shirt, and goes somewhere to rejuvenate and refocus.

Sometimes this takes him to town and at other times to spend a day of romance with the Eastern, cultured school marm, Molly. On one occasion, the Virginian attends a community dance and plays a prank on some of the other attendees.

In a similar, but more dangerous mini vacation, the Pontipee brothers in *Seven Brides for Seven Brothers* overcome one of the worst slumps in movie history by sneaking into town and capturing their seven "brides." In both *The Virginian* and *Seven Brides for Seven Brothers*, the main characters overcome slumps by taking drastic action away from home. It's important not to emulate these exact actions in our day, however, since such pranks and escapades will likely land you in prison. But the movies show us the pattern: time away from the normal routine has the power to break negative slumps.

> **Time away from the normal routine has the power to break negative slumps.**

Likewise, in the 2006 movie *The Holiday*, two women experiencing slumps exchange places between Los Angeles and Surrey, England. Iris (played by Kate Winslet) finds out that the man she has loved for three years is getting married to someone else, and Amanda (played by Cameron Diaz) learns that her live-in boyfriend has been having an affair. To get past their respective slumps, they switch homes while they both seek to regroup and refocus their lives. After numerous dramatic twists and turns that would no doubt impress even Shakespeare, both women make powerful changes, and their new, unusual environments are essential to their success.

Martha's Plan

Such changes frequently occur in real life as well. After another loud argument with her son James, Martha went to her room and cried. Then she fumed. When her husband came home from riding motorcycles with a friend, she told him how frustrated she was with James and his refusal to change. After a long discussion, they agreed that Martha and James simply weren't feeling very bonded and that this problem was going to continue until their levels of trust and empathy drastically improved.

"He just sees me as his annoying disciplinarian," Martha said. Her husband nodded. "And I just see him as ungrateful, stubborn, and immature." She sighed. "And entitled."

They both chuckled.

"The truth is we're both right," Martha said, shaking her head. "I do spend a lot of time telling him what to do and what he can't do, and he really is young and immature...."

After a pause, her husband replied, "You know, so many parents would love to have the problems with their kids that we have with James. No serious issues. He works hard on his studies. He's obedient. He's happy and fun-loving. It's just that he constantly wants to go out with his friends or just lay around before his chores are done, and you don't let him. That always sets him off, and you both get emotional and frustrated."

"But what should I do?" Martha asked.

"First, he doesn't get to disrespect you this way," her husband said. "I'll talk to him. But you need to work it out with him as well, don't you think?"

After more discussion, Martha realized, "As long as we're doing the same thing over and over, this just isn't going to click for either of us. It's too easy to fall back into our habit of arguing. We need a change of scenery."

Three days later, Martha, James, and his little sister Kristin left home early in the morning for a quick trip to San Diego. As they pulled out of Scottsdale, Martha announced, "I know I told you this was going to be a surprise, but now that we're on the road, does anyone want to know where we're headed?"

"Yes!" Kristen exclaimed.

James grinned. "Yeah, tell us, Mom."

"Okay, we're going to SeaWorld!"

"Cool!"

"Really?"

"Yes, really."

"Why?" Kristen asked curiously. "We've never done something like this before, so on the spur of the moment. Why now?"

"Actually, I have this stack of audios that I want to listen to, and I need to get away for a couple of days to do it. I thought we'd all enjoy SeaWorld, and it gives me a chance to listen to these and bond with both of you at the same time. Will you pick which one we listen to first?" Martha asked James, handing him the stack.

"Sure." He looked through the titles and asked, "How long are these?"

"Less than an hour each, I think," she responded. "It's about a six-hour drive from Phoenix to San Diego, so we should be able to listen to all ten of these before we get back home."

"Cool!" Kristen said, rifling through the pile, reading the titles.

James wanted to listen to a different audio than Kristen did, so they played Rock-Paper-Scissors. James won, and Martha put in his selection. As they drove and listened, they occasionally paused the audio and discussed what they were learning. At first, James acted bored, but he warmed to the project as they kept listening. The talk was funny, interesting, and deep.

After lunch, they returned to the car and got back on the road. "I get to pick which one we listen to this time," Kristen announced.

A little more than forty-eight hours later, after a fun day together at SeaWorld and an evening at the beach in Coronado, they arrived back home in the midafternoon. They had listened to audios all the way to San Diego, but they spent the drive home talking about their fun trip and only listened to one more.

As they neared Phoenix, Martha said, "I wonder if you two can help me with something?"

"What is it?" Kristen asked.

"Well," Martha replied, "I have loved this time together. We're having so much fun. I keep finding myself wondering how we can keep this feeling once we're home. Do you guys have any ideas?"

They talked for the rest of the drive, and James mentioned that he needed a better attitude about his chores. Martha asked, "What can I do to help you with that?"

"Nothing," James said. "Dad and I talked about it, and I'm just going to do better."

And he did. He wasn't perfect at it, and Martha and James still had the tendency to argue a little when they butted heads. But he did much better than before the trip. Martha found it easier to remain calm, and James did a better job of just obeying when she asked him to finish his chores.

"Why do you think the trip helped so much?" her husband asked as they discussed it two weeks later.

"I'm not exactly sure. Your talk with him helped. And maybe it's just that we both feel more connected now. Or maybe it was the talks we had during the drive about both of us doing better. Whatever it is, I like it."

Mini Success!

There is something powerful about getting out of your usual routine, filling your time for a couple of days with positive words, ideas, stories, and feelings from the right kind of

> **There is something powerful about getting out of your usual routine.**

books and audios and just rejuvenating. It brings more focus.

Whatever the challenge, this rung is very effective. So if you're in a rut, take a mini vacation, and make sure you fill it with positive input and thoughts from excellent books and audios as well as your true life Dreams and Motivations.

> **Having a mini success gets you back on the right track fast.**

Having a mini success gets you back on the right track fast.

Auditory Revolution

Audios are extremely helpful in this process. In a special issue on ideas for improving our society, *Time* magazine presented an article entitled:

THE IDEAS ISSUE:
TRAVEL
TAKE YOUR **EARS** ON VACATION

In this article, the author suggested that, "Being a 'Sound Tourist' can help us get more out of travel—and help reveal sonic delights in our everyday lives....In travel guides you will find descriptions of beautiful vistas and iconic architecture to look at

> **The right kind of two-day mini vacation is a powerful, effective slump buster.**

but very little about sounds. What a shame."[11]

He points out that given current audio technology, "we are entering a golden age of sound tourism."[12] Listening to excellent audios while we travel, or even just take a mental vacation, for a day or two is part of this.

The right kind of two-day mini vacation is a powerful, effective slump buster.

Questions

Q: Should you take the kids?

A: Maybe. Maybe not. Just make sure you will be able to listen to a passel of great audios, read great books, and also have time to think.

Q: Should you invite your spouse?

A: It depends. If you'll end up whining about your slump all day, then no, go alone. But if your spouse wants to listen to excellent audios with you and talk together about your respective Dreams, then great. Sometimes you will want to take your vacation alone, so trust that feeling. Other times, having your spouse along will make your trip a lot more fun and effective.

Q: Should you go all out, spend a lot, and make it a major event?

A: Perhaps. But two days is the right length for most Slump-to-Success vacations. More or less than this tends to be a lot less effective. You certainly don't have to take the expensive route. Packing sandwiches from home and listening to your audios and reading books at the park for two full days can be one of the best vacations of your life—if the audios and books get enough attention. Take off your shoes and walk in the grass with bare feet. Lie in the grass and look up at the sky while you listen. Watch the breeze in the trees.

If you're so inclined and can afford it, a nice hotel or a flight to a sunny beach, mountain fly-fishing streams, or the like can have real appeal as well. These details are less important than making sure you think deeply about your Dreams and have some fun. Don't use debt because this choice almost always adds to the feeling of slump.

Q: Should you take your work with you?

A: Absolutely not. If you're asking this question, you probably don't know what the word *vacation* means, and you need to read the book *A Month of Italy* by Chris Brady. Soon. In fact, this is a great book to take with you and read during any mini vacation.

Not understanding how to vacation is a serious source of slumps. Periodic longer vacations like the one described in *A Month of Italy* can help you avoid slumps in the first place.

Q: Should you take your phone with you?

A: No, except as a safety issue and if not being available for an important call means you can't take your vacation right away. If this is the case, keep your phone off except during the few minutes you're using it for safety or the important call. Your goal is to get away from your familiar routine, and fielding calls or talking on the phone are about as familiar as it gets for most people.

Q: Is there anything else you should know about this two-day vacation?

A: Yes. Don't let the audios and books get in the way of fun. Do fun first, as much as possible. Truly decompress. After all, a big part of most slumps is just built up stress.

> **Fun is a powerful positive!**

Think about your Dreams, and fill the rest of the time with fun, reading, and listening. Fun is a powerful positive, and it will have similar anti-slump benefits to those of the good audios and books.

Vacation, Vacation, Vacation!

Whereas the motto in real estate is "location, location, location," for slump busting, it's "vacation, vacation, vacation." Remember, they don't call it a vacation for nothing. The verb *vacation* is defined by the *Compact Oxford English Dictionary* as:

the action of leaving a place or job

That's your goal. To break the pattern and get away from the place in which the slump is growing and flourishing. To go somewhere else and do something else so the slump has to fight to stay alive in the new surroundings and against your higher level of focus.

The word *vacation* also carries the connotation of "holiday, trip, tour, break, mini-break; leave, time off, recess, furlough..." as outlined in the *Compact Oxford Thesaurus*. To repeat, the point is to get away from the places and actions that have allowed the slump to take hold, to put yourself in a new environment for a couple days, to reboot your creativity and positivity, and to focus on what really, truly matters most to you.

This is powerful. Vacations can be "learning vacations," "romantic vacations," "recuperative vacations," "fun vacations," "summer vacations," "family vacations," "annual vacations," full-blown "sabbaticals," and so on.

The common thread is to get out of your current routine and experience something different for a time. As for this anti-slump mini vacation, your focus is to reboot and redirect.

Have fun? Yes.

Be romantic? Sure.

Learn something? Great.

Just relax? Absolutely.

But above all, when you get back home, you want to be different. You want to return to your house with lots of positive words ringing in your ears and with your Dreams and Motivations foremost in your mind.

> **Just the act of absorbing truly positive audios and books from the right sources is a "vacation."**

That's a slump-killing vacation. It's not a perfect utopia

because you still have to go back to real life, but it's the kind of vacation that truly helps you climb the Ladder toward more success and increased happiness.

Actually, just the act of absorbing truly positive audios and books from the right sources is a "vacation." It transports your thoughts to a different place and routine, that of hearing and thinking about what the speakers and authors are teaching.

> **The words we read and hear from great leaders are an excellent vacation from the more routine things we usually hear and think about in everyday life.**

Words are powerful. They have meaning. The words we read and hear from great leaders about facing challenges, working toward success, overcoming setbacks, setting and achieving goals, serving others, and so on, are an excellent vacation from the more routine things we usually hear and think about in everyday life. And the lessons you learn from the books you read and the audios you listen to will give you ideas for implementing your plans.

The Event

Sometimes we have the opportunity to attend a seminar and hear great messages from proven leaders in person. This can provide some of the most powerful slump-killing and slump-proofing experiences of all. If a workshop or seminar of interest to you coincides with your need for a slump-fighting vacation, great! Such an event may last more than two days, but the higher energy of participating with other people who are also seeking increased success will definitely be worth it.

Whatever else happens, when a slump comes, the right kind of mini vacation is the perfect response — after you've taken action to outline your Dreams and Motivations. It puts the excitement back into your life, and it returns you to your house a new, better person. It's a huge step up the Ladder away from a slump.

WORD OF THE DAY

Utopia: "paradise, heaven, heaven on earth, Eden, Garden of Eden, Shangri-La, Elysium; idyll, nirvana, ideal place."

(Compact Oxford Thesaurus)

Wash on Monday, Iron on Tuesday,
Mend on Wednesday, Churn on Thursday,
Clean on Friday, Bake on Saturday,
Rest on Sunday.
—LAURA INGALLS WILDER,
LITTLE HOUSE IN THE BIG WOODS

RUNG 5: NAIL THE FIRST DAY AFTER YOUR VACATION
(AND THE NEXT WEEK AND MONTH)

All's well that ends well.
—POPULARIZED BY JOHN HEYWOOD,
ENGLISH PLAYWRIGHT, IN 1546

The measure of success for your anti-slump mini vacation is how you feel and act after you get home. As you decided before your trip, the instant you arrive home, your slump is over. Act like it. Think like it. Chris Brady teaches, "It's not a vacation if it doesn't end, so close it out with courage."

Once you're back home, keep listening to positive audios and reading great books to maintain your upbeat thoughts and attitude, and keep refreshing your Dreams and Motivations in the morning and evening as well as at mealtime.

Moreover, on the first day after your vacation, start doing everything on your To-Do List (the projects and tasks that you need to do to achieve your goals), and don't stop for at least a month! If you do these powerful steps, any slump will become an excellent opportunity to reevaluate your top goals, outline what you need to do to really succeed, and refresh your focus.

> **"It's not a vacation if it doesn't end, so close it out with courage."**
> **— Chris Brady**

What happens the first day back from the getaway is very important. Here is the vital checklist:

- Read your Dreams and Motivations first thing in the morning…and again at breakfast.
- Listen to at least three hours of positive, excellent audios (the earlier in the day, the better, in most cases).
- Read your Dreams and Motivations at lunch.
- Do all the items on your To-Do List.
- Spend some time working on the new opportunity that has come into your life!
- Read your Dreams and Motivations at dinner…and again right before you go to bed.

Be sure that you do every item on your To-Do List. This is simply essential. Without it, you'll almost surely start allowing yourself to fall back into old routines and habits, the very things that got you into a slump. Now that the slump is officially over, your important work must replace your old routines and patterns—every day, especially your first day back to your normal life...and the first week and month.

> **Now that the slump is officially over, your important work must replace your old routines and patterns.**

The Special Thing

There are at least three reasons your decision to follow through on your plan is so crucial. The first, as mentioned above, is that having integrity in implementing your To-Do List will naturally replace old, negative patterns that brought you down before and could easily do so again. You'll experience real change.

> **Integrity in implementing your To-Do List will naturally replace old, negative patterns that brought you down before.**

Second, your To-Do List exists because you feel that it will bring about your one-year goals and five-year dreams. If you don't dutifully use your To-Do List, it's unlikely you'll have what you want in 365 days or in sixty months. Of course, you'll want to adjust your list as needed, but truly following through on it is an essential part of success.

These choices are among those small, simple things that the world calls "secrets" but great leaders simply call "habits." Do them. Your To-Do List is your power. You can either select low power, mediocre power, high power, or great power. To choose great power, always implement and improve upon your To-Do List whenever possible.

Third, consistently and effectively living your To-Do List every day of every week and always improving upon it will make you part of the 5 percent. The consequences of this are almost impossible to overstate. You will live your greatest Dreams, you will serve many, and you will find success and happiness.

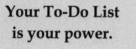

Your To-Do List is your power.

In short, this one small decision will largely determine your life's trajectory.

Ironically, most people in the 95 percent find reasons to justify not making this choice. Some even criticize those who make it. This is ironic because such criticisms and justifications guarantee that those making them remain part of the 95 percent. The 5 percent reject these distractions, focusing instead on consistently doing the right things.

People who stick with this "road less travelled" are rare. It leads to greatness, but too few people fully grasp or embrace it. As bestselling author Nassim Taleb pointed out, this is the root of America's greatness. This is also the foundation of Britain's success as a leading influence of Western Civilization.

In a nutshell, as Taleb argued in his book *Antifragile*, America's "principal asset" isn't its universities or its other institutions but a very special facet of freedom: the fact that in this culture there is comparatively little shame in taking risks, aiming for great things, failing and starting over, and repeating the process until great success is achieved.[14]

In many other cultures around the world, the opposite is true: the shame of any failure is so high that hardly anyone is willing to aim for big things.[15]

As a result, for the past two centuries, people in the North American and Western European nations have inno- vated at much higher rates than their peers in other parts of the world. This has spurred social progress and created today's enviable Western economic prosperity. The nations where more citizens take risks and have the freedoms to keep striving to fulfill their goals see more successes than those with fewer innovators or freedoms.

> **The nations where more citizens take risks and have the freedoms to keep striving to fulfill their goals see more successes than those with fewer innovators or freedoms.**

Western Civilization in general, and North America specifically, are currently facing significant decline precisely because the shame level associated with entre- preneurial risks and struggles is rising in Euro-American society. This is both sad and surprising! Why would we reject the very things that made our nations so successful?

Interestingly, this increase in shame coincides with a reduction in general faith, particularly the application of faith in our educational and working lives. As many people more frequently tend to separate personal faith from their schooling and careers, they are much less likely to take risks, even positive ones.

There are many ways this presents itself in our current culture. For example, as college has become more expected in the population, non-innovative careers on the "normal" path, focused on a steady paycheck and guaranteed benefits, have become a new definition of success. Many Western parents now idealize these things for their children rather than the higher (but more risky) goals of major innovation, sacrificing to contribute and serve, or top leadership.

Yet, as Taleb insists, risk taking and the freedom to pursue huge successes, despite the risks, remains America's most important asset,[16] the source of its continued success and prosperity. If America or any other nation ever ceases to encourage and reward innovators, it will soon cease to be great.

One way to look at this is illustrated in the following diagram. A society that attaches shame to aiming high and engaging personal risk in the pursuit of great things, working hard and struggling, failing or facing setbacks, or learning from the process and starting over with the same or even greater goals has a familiar negative look:

Such cultures can accurately be called "societies of perpetual slump." In contrast, consider the same process in a nation where parents, grandparents, and other community leaders consider the following to be the pattern of success, leadership, and progress:

- Aiming high, even in the face of personal risk
- Working hard and struggling
- Failing or facing setbacks
- Learning from the process and starting over with the same or even greater goals

This is the hero's path, the pattern of real success. It might be diagrammed:

Nations, as well as individuals and groups, typically adopt one or the other of these attitudes. If you experience a slump, one of two things is certain: (1) You need to be much more consistent in implementing your Game Plan (your list of goals for achieving your Dreams) and/or your To-Do List (tasks to help you achieve your goals), or (2) You need to brainstorm, research, ponder and pray, or work with mentors to find ways to improve your Game Plan and/or To-Do List.

This is true at both the individual level and the national level.

Sadly, many people in modern times are afraid of risk. They teach their children to avoid risk. They fail to teach them how to wisely assess it, determine how to manage it, and effectively engage it when needed to achieve important things that really matter. Current generations are being widely trained to run from risk, to always take the easy route or the safest course, and not to take chances.

> **Innovation is the path to progress, success, leadership, and advancement.**

This amounts to teaching our society to stop innovating. As Taleb suggested, the first step of innovation is to get into some trouble, "serious trouble" but not "terminal." And both trouble and innovation create some discomfort. As Orrin Woodward put it, "If everyone agrees with you, you're not innovating."

Yet innovation is the path to progress. It's the path to success, leadership, and advancement. If you don't innovate, you don't need to lead—you can simply follow a road already marked by others. Leadership requires innovation, and innovation is the work of leaders.

> **Leadership requires innovation, and innovation is the work of leaders.**

Innovation is the material of success, and a certain amount of wise, well-chosen risk is its necessary ally. These two—intelligent risk and innovation—are the double helix in the DNA of leadership and progress. Without them, things stagnate or devolve.

All of this makes our current society's trajectory even more tragic. In a culture where risk for great achievement and contribution has long been held in high esteem, we are changing the rules, telling the rising generations that they should avoid "reaching for the stars" and instead settle for the "normal" path, as long as it includes very little risk, a college degree, and a steady job. The fact that degrees no longer bring any job at all for over half of college graduates is ignored.

We are undermining a traditionally entrepreneurial society (that blesses us all with relative freedom and opportunities for prosperity) by teaching the youth that "the system" is the answer. In the words of bestselling author Oliver DeMille, we've bought in to "the conveyor belt." Or as Taleb put it, we are "lecturing birds on how to fly."[17] With enough such lectures, the rising generations are increasingly less interested in flying at all. We are sowing the seeds, and indeed now beginning to harvest the crops, of a serious Societal Slump.

> As you become a leader, you'll naturally reduce the effects of the Societal Slump and help others do the same.

The most effective antidote is for you to become proficient at overcoming every personal slump you encounter. As you become a leader, you'll naturally reduce the effects of the Societal Slump and help others do the same.

The Main Action

Note that most people who find themselves in a personal slump are likely struggling with #1 (inconsistent application of their Game Plan) and #2 (needing to fan the flames of their Dreams). When you get home from your mini vacation, immediately pour your heart and efforts into implementing your Game Plan. This is the surest path to post-slump success. To *all* success, in fact.

Few things are more personally energizing than taking the time to outline your Game Plan and then consistently reading it and applying it—especially the To-Do List. This is action! It is also the right, and best, kind of action when you are faced with a slump.

Action has a way of fixing things—much more than

> **Action has a way of fixing things.**

inaction—and your To-Do List contains the most important actions you can take. Indeed, if you ever discover something more important, add it to your To-Do List right away.

This is Rung 5 on the Slump-to-Success Ladder. The moment you get home from your two-day vacation, your slump is over. Immediately begin implementing your To-Do List.

Do the same thing day after day for the first week. Then do it for a full month.

If you do less than this, you'll open yourself to the dangerous potential of falling back into your slump. If you stay with your Game Plan faithfully for a full month, the slump will usually be broken. You'll have to keep doing the Game Plan—including needed adjustments—to keep slumps away in the future, of course.

Great leaders know that to keep on the path of success, they need to exert integrity every day by knowing and doing the truly important things. This is a proven and extremely effective secret, well, *principle*, of great success, and it works!

WORD OF THE DAY

energize: "enliven, lighten up, animate, vitalize, invigorate, perk up, excite, electrify…, fire up, rouse, motivate, move…, encourage, galvanize…"

(Compact Oxford Thesaurus)

Instead of having hope, we've resorted
[as a society] to diversions...
sports...drinking...TV...[18]
—George Guzzardo

RUNG 6: BEWARE THE BIG "A"

Things fall apart; the centre cannot hold...
—W. B. Yeats, "The Second Coming"

In Nathaniel Hawthorne's classic novel *The Scarlet Letter*, the heroine, Hester Prynne, wears a large letter "A" on her dress to signify that she has been found guilty of adultery. In our day, there is also a big "A," and it frequently shows up during any slump we experience. This "A" stands for "Addiction."

There is something about being in a slump that naturally tempts us to give in to addictions. In the field of psychology, this is often referred to as "escapism," or the use of addictive behaviors to try to escape our slumps and slumped feelings.

Such addictive behaviors, including gambling, drinking alcohol excessively, watching online pornography, abusing prescription medication and pain killers or self-prescribed over-the-counter drugs, hoarding, and so on can be hurtful and damaging. Escapist addictions can also be more mild, such as trying to drown our sorrows or anxieties in enough Dr. Pepper or Cherry Lime Coke or seeking a break from our slump-induced sadness after a romantic breakup or career letdown by stuffing ourselves with boxes of maple donuts or tubs of raspberry chocolate truffles.

In current times, as mentioned in *Psychology Today*, one of the most prevalent types of using addictions in an attempt to escape our stresses is to bury ourselves in electronic distraction or commiseration through Facebook, blogs, YouTube, Pinterest, television, video games, cell phones, and various social media platforms.[19]

Playing games for endless hours, living every second with music playing in the background, or watching a marathon of old *Smallville* reruns are the go-to escapes for many people. And while electronic escapism may be less damaging than substance addiction, any addictive behavior has the potential to do more than turn a little slump into a Life Slump. It also does the opposite of the Ladder: it transforms a slump into fewer and fewer successes ahead.

Note that distraction itself is a powerful addiction. Chris Brady wrote:

There are so many things to capture our attention and affection [that] we are in constant danger of being sidetracked. Many a good intention has ended in obscurity, many a great leader has fallen to distraction, many a great book remains partially-written, many a musical composition is still unfinished, and many a goal has gone unachieved. These are the casualties of distraction, and their tally would fill all the ledger books in the world....

Distraction to an adult with a goal is a lot like a shiny object on the side of a path to a toddler. It doesn't matter what the distraction *is*; it only matters that it *glitters*.[20]

People also find escapist addictions in things like eating sugary treats, complaining and gossiping with friends, surfing online for endless hours, wasting days following a long list of celebrities on Twitter, writing mean comments about other people on social media sites, watching every new Vine that comes along, and shopping/finding ways to run up credit card balances on needless consumer goods and services.

This latter behavior is known in pop culture as "retail therapy," but it can be an escapist addiction nonetheless. Likewise, as Claude Hamilton teaches, addiction to buying lottery tickets doesn't make you happy, even if you win.[21]

> **As Claude Hamilton teaches, addiction to buying lottery tickets doesn't make you happy, even if you win.**

Stages of the Big "A"

The four stages of escapism are the same as the stages of addiction: (1) the initial release of short-term "enjoyment," (2) avoidance of important issues and responsibilities in life, (3) full-blown neglect of the people and tasks that really matter, and (4) obsession with the addiction.[22] Of course, all four stages will deepen and lengthen any slump.

> **Every time a slump arrives, it also brings a great opportunity with it.**

Again, whenever a slump comes, so does a temptation to get caught in escapist behaviors and to let them turn into addictions. Fortunately, as mentioned in earlier chapters, every time a slump arrives, it also brings a great opportunity with it.

This is powerful knowledge. If a slump comes, it always brings this forked path: the temptation of escapist behaviors on the one hand and a great opportunity for increased levels of success on the other.

A key to success, to leadership, to greatness, is to consistently reject the Big "A" and always focus on the Dream:

$$\text{Success in a Slump} = \frac{\underline{\textbf{Big Dream + Rejection of Big "A"}}}{\textbf{Consistency}}$$

Rung 6 is extremely important. When a slump comes, beware the Big "A." Don't give any energy to escapist behaviors or addictions, even so-called "little" ones. Reject escapist, addictive temptations 100 percent.

Societal Slump

In addition, we can learn a lot about what not to do from an interesting source: government. Note that governments nearly always do the wrong things when they find themselves in a slump. They immediately jump into addictive behaviors.

For example, study a period of major national slump or crisis, and you'll almost always find governments responding with escapist addictions such as increased spending and debt as well as printing fiat, inflationary currency. When a war takes place, this is how most governments react. When an economic downturn occurs, they make this same unwise choice.

This model is as old as governments. As Orrin Woodward wrote in *RESOLVED: 13 Resolutions for LIFE*:

[I]n 1690…[t]he soldiers arrived back in Boston, ill-tempered and demanding their salaries regardless of the failed outcome of the raid. Hosting discontented soldiers who had weapons and the will to use them, was not an enjoyable experience for the Boston citizens.

And after their attempt to raise the funds to pay the soldiers through local merchants were rejected, the government leaders struck upon an idea that still echoes today. The Massachusetts State government concluded that printing £7,000 of paper notes to pay the soldiers was safer than having unpaid soldiers within the city.

Concerned that the public would not accept the paper, the government made several pledges in an attempt to alleviate the public's suspicion…. It took less than four months for more notes to be issued...[and by] February of 1691, another £40,000 of unbacked paper notes was issued to make up for a shortage of government funds. Politicians proclaimed boldly, and falsely, that this would be the last issue of notes....

Not surprisingly, the politicians, feeling the Midas touch, dipped into the well again and again, multiplying the fiat money nearly seven times in just one year. [This led to massive inflation that was shut down only when London intervened.][23]

This is what happens — to governments, businesses, or individuals — when a slump turns into escapist and addictive behaviors. Things get much worse quickly.

Repeating the Escapist Pattern

The United States repeated this addiction after the Revolutionary War, after the Civil War, and again after World War I. In every case, doing so helped turn a more minor slump into a major recession or full-blown economic depression. Many other governments have made the same mistake.

> **When you experience a slump and choose an escapist Big "A," the consequence is a much worse slump or depression.**

The lesson is clear: when you experience a slump and choose an escapist Big "A," the consequence is a much worse slump or depression.

Along with spending addictions, governments frequently go on regulation binges as well. In an economic slump, the quickest solution to the problem is innovation. However, higher regulation nearly always slows the rate of innovation. In other words, the worst thing a government can do in a slump is to increase its regulatory footprint. And yet, this is exactly what governments do.

It's downright shocking how unwise this is. But, it shouldn't be too surprising when you really think about it. After all, the worst thing an individual can do in a slump is sit on the couch and gorge on hot fudge sundaes or cans of cheese whiz. Yet that is exactly what some people do.

Choose the Ladder instead. Reject escapist, addictive choices outright, immediately, and consistently, no matter how little they may seem. As a leader, your path is the Ladder, with its six powerful rungs, not any kind of addiction.

Lessons from a Mini Summit

This parallel between governments and individuals experiencing a slump and turning to escapist addictions is all too real. In fact, we can learn a great deal from this.

Today's governments are as prone as those in history to turning a slump into a bigger crisis simply by resorting to

> Today's governments are as prone as those in history to turning a slump into a bigger crisis simply by resorting to addictive behaviors, especially unwise economic and monetary choices.

addictive behaviors, especially unwise economic and monetary choices. For example, in a recent summit, three thinkers addressed the way current governments in North America and Western Europe are responding to a challenging international economic slump.

The participants already knew that the history of government responses to economic challenges is usually to make bad, addictive monetary decisions. As discussed above, this was done in colonial and later revolutionary America by printing and distributing fiat money. Historically, this has always led to major inflation and increased economic downturns.

Then, in the 1930s, the US government took this to a new level by ending the Gold Standard. Not only did the slump worsen, but it quickly deteriorated into the Great Depression.

Between the 1940s and the 1980s, the Federal Reserve used interest rates and money supply in an attempt to protect the economy from a similar crash. But this policy became less and less effective during the 1990s and 2000s, leading to the Great Recession that began in 2008. The government response was massive taxpayer bailouts of government and private sector entities, further borrowing, and increased printing of fiat, inflationary currency.

To mask what was happening, the experts used terms few people understood, like "QE1," "QE3," and "quantitative easing." Sounds good, doesn't it? After all, it must be "easing" something for us. Actually, all it "eased" was the pressure on our currency to be worth more, to buy more. It eased the value of our currency, making each dollar worth less.

With interest rates on most savings accounts and many investments hovering below 1 percent, the Federal Reserve really couldn't use lower interest rates to try to help the economy. In a sad struggle to feed their addiction to more ready government money, economists searched for other ways to get their fix. Again, this resulted in increased borrowing and even more federal spending. Amazing!

> **Slumps tempt us to engage addictions, and if we do, the addictions take over and cause even worse slumps.**

Slumps tempt us to engage addictions, and if we do, the addictions take over and cause even worse slumps. Perhaps by understanding how obvious this is when looking at government behaviors, we will realize how true it is for us as individuals as well.

WORD OF THE DAY

endeavor: "try, attempt, seek, undertake, aspire, aim, set out; strive, struggle, labor, toil, work, exert yourself, do your best, do your utmost, give your all..."

(Compact Oxford Thesaurus)

It possesses possibilities—both
towards danger and success.
—WINSTON CHURCHILL

MAKE SURE YOUR LADDER IS LEANING AGAINST THE RIGHT WALL

Actions speak louder than words.
—ENGLISH PROVERB POPULARIZED BY MARK TWAIN

So far, we've learned about the Six Rungs of the Slump-to-Success Ladder:

- **Rung 1:** When a slump hits, take action! Get off the couch and get going.

- **Rung 2:** Plan the right kind of two-day mini vacation.

- **Rung 3:** Release the power of your Dreams and Motivations.

- **Rung 4:** Let your slump roll on a two-day vacation filled with positive thoughts, the right kind of books and audios, the Dream, and fun.

- **Rung 5:** Nail the first day, week, and month after your mini vacation.

- **Rung 6:** Beware the tempting Big "A" of escapist addictions.

The Slump-to-Success Ladder is powerful. And, ultimately, it hinges on two key choices: (1) to initiate and take action and (2) to make your Dreams come alive.

This second choice is essential. If you don't get your Dreams and Motivations right, the rest of your hard work won't bring the results you're really seeking. Climbing the Ladder is great, but, in the words of Orrin Woodward, "Make sure your ladder is leaning against the right wall!"

If it isn't, you'll do all the work, give all your heart and effort to the challenge, and climb the Ladder with blood, sweat, tears, and sacrifice, only to arrive at the top and realize you climbed the wrong wall. Not a good place to be!

Obviously, you want to scale the right wall, not the wrong one. But how? This is a very important question.

The answer is clear. Start with the right Dreams and Motivations and then the right Game Plan and actions. This means making sure that your life Dream is all it should be and all it can be.

This is a serious reality because with your focus targeted on the Dream as you climb the Ladder, you need to be sure your Game Plan is also right. If you get this wrong, you'll get the whole thing wrong. Talk about a slump!

Again, just imagine putting years of work into your goals, struggling against the odds, climbing, facing and overcoming challenges, dealing with criticism and opposition, working, working, working, and finally arriving victorious at the top of your Ladder and then looking around and realizing that you don't like what you've earned and won.

> **It's important to develop a great Game Plan to achieve your Dream. This ensures that your climb up the Ladder will get you where you want to be.**

In short, it's important to develop a great Game Plan to achieve your Dream. This ensures that your climb up the Ladder will get you where you want to be.

The Right Goals

Let's begin with goals. In an earlier chapter, we started with your Dreams and Motivations. That's enough to help you turn a slump into positives, but to really get the Game Plan right, you'll need a longer-term goal as well.

Specifically:

- What is your life goal, your life purpose, your life mission?
- When you pass away some day, how do you want people to remember you?
- What do you want people to remember about the things you did, your relationships, your personality, your service, and your accomplishments?

These questions help you go deeper into your Dream, Cause, Calling, and Legacy. Knowing the answer to these questions is very helpful. They can assist you in staying focused on what's really important as you progress through life. And when a slump comes, they will immediately give you clarity on the Game Plan. Knowing your purpose helps you remain grounded, even when things are difficult.

> **Knowing your purpose helps you remain grounded, even when things are difficult.**

If you are unclear on your long-term, major life purpose, take some time right now to ponder, search your heart, seek God's purpose for you, and write your life mission down in a place you can review it daily.

Add this to your Dreams and Motivations page if it's not already there.

Alignment

Now, with this step accomplished, review the other parts of your Game Plan. Is there anything you'd like to change, or improve, in your five-year goals, one-year plans, or weekly or daily To-Do Lists?

Also, do they align, meaning, if you truly implement your weekly and daily lists, will these naturally lead to success in your one-year plans? And will your one-year plans naturally support your five-year and long-term goals?

If there is any way to improve these, do so. Include these with your written Game Plan that you review every day.

This process of reviewing and improving your Game Plan is something to repeat frequently throughout your life. Your purpose and long-term goals likely won't change much, but as mentioned, more immediate plans and lists should be adjusted as often as necessary. In fact, every slump

> **Every slump is really a wake-up call, telling you that it's time to revisit your Game Plan and make sure you're on track.**

is really a wake-up call telling you that it's time to revisit your Game Plan and make sure you're on track.

As you do this, always look for ways to improve the Game Plan.

Help with Goals

One of the best primers on goals is Brian Tracy's book *Goals!* Tracy includes the following guidelines for setting and achieving the right goals in life. Read each of these carefully and ponder them:

- Decide upon your major definite purpose.
- Measure your progress.
- Remove the roadblocks.
- Associate with the right people.
- Make a plan of action.
- Manage your time well.
- Review your goals daily.
- Visualize your goals continually.
- Persist until you succeed.[24]
- Follow the leaders, not the followers.[25]

Use each these things to improve your Game Plan. This is a powerful outline for establishing and achieving effective goals. Each suggestion on this list will help you polish your Game Plan and implement it more consistently.

Vision Counts

It's important here to clarify that we shouldn't get caught up on the specific word choice of *goals*. The truth is that some people hear the word *goals* and tense up in fear, like students who hear the word *test* and shut down, even though they knew the answers to the questions before the scary word *exam*, *quiz*, or *test* was used.

> **Visualize, imagine, and dream. Then write your dreams down and read over them frequently.**

If you are one of those people who sometimes feel a bit anxious about goals, relax. Just visualize what you want in your life and where you want to be in five years. That's all we're talking about. Visualize, imagine, and dream.

Change the term *Game Plan* to *Visualization Plan*, if it helps. They're equally effective because they're ultimately the same thing. But write your Dreams down on paper and read over them frequently. Don't worry about the semantics; just accept the benefit of the powerful Game Plan or Visualization Plan.

Another critique of goals adds the valid point that some people achieve more effectively by focusing on daily, weekly, and monthly behaviors and actions rather than emphasizing distant Dreams and goals. This works for some people.

Whatever your long-term goals, without quality, consistent actions on a daily basis, success will always remain elusive. Some people do best by focusing on the daily actions instead of longer-term plans or goals. But in truth, most people find that using all three of these tools (Goals/Visions, Plans, and To-Do Lists) brings the best results.

Real Tools

Successful people, the 5 percent, find that long-term purpose and direction, intermediate-term strategies, and shorter-term measurement of real daily actions all help them become better leaders. Without such tools, everyone struggles to achieve genuine success, and most people struggle even more in a time of slump.

As Thomas J. Watson, an iconic historical CEO of IBM, reportedly said, "If you want to achieve excellence, you can get there today. As of this second, quit doing less-than-excellent work." This is sage advice for every time in our lives, including during a slump. Excellence is its own reward, and it quickly invites many slump-busting thoughts, feelings, and behaviors.

> Excellence is its own reward, and it quickly invites many slump-busting thoughts, feelings, and behaviors.

To summarize, make sure your Dream and Game Plan are right. There is power in the Ladder. When you climb it, you not only rise out of a slump; you also set in motion new successes, increased ripples of progress, and positive change. This will make a huge difference in your future and the future of those you serve and influence. Before you climb the Ladder, just make sure it is leaning against the right wall!

WORD OF THE DAY

excellence: "quality, superiority, brilliance, greatness, merit, caliber..., virtuosity, accomplishment, mastery..."

(Compact Oxford Thesaurus)

THE THREE L'S OF LIFE AND LEADERSHIP

Live, love, laugh…
— Bessie Anderson Stanley,
American Poet, 1904

In times of slump and in other times—always in fact—remember to focus on what really matters. This is a great principle of both happiness and success. Those who live it every day will be in a better place to smile in the face of a slump and to quickly get to work climbing the Ladder of increased success.

Among the most important things that really matter are the great verbs "live, love, and laugh." These Three Ls are not little issues. They are huge. For leaders, for those who are part of the 5 percent, these three words are a profound way of life.

The combination of these three words in this popular order came from a modern proverb penned in 1904 by poet Bessie Anderson Stanley, but most people don't know the story behind these three words, even though they are now widely posted on bumper stickers, wall plaques, and websites. The name of Stanley's poem was, appropriately, "Success." Consider each important idea as you read her powerful expression of lasting wisdom:

He has achieved success who has lived well, laughed often, and loved much;

who has enjoyed the trust of pure women, the respect of intelligent men and the love of little children;

who has filled his niche and accomplished his task;

who has left the world better than he found it whether by an improved poppy, a perfect poem or a rescued soul;

who has never lacked appreciation of Earth's beauty or failed to express it;

who has always looked for the best in others and given them the best he had;

whose life was an inspiration; whose memory a benediction.

Real leaders are on the vanguard of promoting these very things in the world. That's what leaders do. They do these things when times are good, and they do them when times are hard. In success and in a slump, for better or for worse, great leaders do what really matters.

> **In success and in a slump, for better or for worse, great leaders do what really matters.**

Balance vs. Excellence

Moreover, each leader knows that he or she has a main purpose in life and that achieving this purpose is the real definition of success. Sometimes this ideal, the concept of effectively fulfilling one's life purpose and simultaneously doing the important things—including living, loving, and laughing—is called *balance*.

Using this word too often teaches a set of falsehoods, however, because a search for balance can communicate that nobody should be too great at anything, that we should tone down our strengths as well as our weaknesses. A better word for great leadership is *excellence*.

This word shift puts the focus on doing great things as you seek your life purpose.

> **Whereas *balance* can be defined as mediocrity in everything, *excellence* can only occur if you seek it in multiple facets of your daily experience.**

Whereas *balance* can be defined as mediocrity in everything, *excellence* can only occur if you seek it in multiple facets of your daily experience.

When a slump comes into a person's life, excellence is a powerful and effective antidote. In fact, consider the strength of applying excellence to each of the Six Rungs:

1. Take *excellent* action!
2. Plan an *excellent*, slump-killing mini vacation.
3. Refocus on or develop a truly *excellent* life's Dream.
4. Vacation with *excellent* books and audios, and let the *excellence* immerse your mind with quality.
5. Apply your Game Plan every day with *excellent* consistency. Don't miss a day! This is integrity.
6. Choose the opportunity that comes with every slump over all escapist temptations. This is always, always, the *excellent* choice, and it leads to increased *excellence*.

> **When a slump comes into a person's life, excellence is a powerful and effective antidote.**

Make sure your Ladder is leaning against the right wall, an *excellent* wall, and make sure you love excellently, laugh excellently, and live excellently.

One More Wrinkle

In all of this, also remember that some slumps are predictable. For example, it has become part of modern culture to expect a midlife crisis somewhere in each person's forties. Youth is often seen as a time of growth and social experience sprinkled with various victories and excitement about the future. The twenties are viewed as a time of fun and achievement and the thirties as a decade of hard work and, hopefully, promotions.

But many people now expect the decade of their forties to be punctuated with setbacks or surprises. These can come in the health, relationships, and career arenas, among others. Words associated with this time of life frequently include: discontentment, apathy, frustration, dissatisfaction, blame, gloomy, and stress.

Sad.

Likewise, some people say that most marriages face a "seven-year itch" or other natural slumps. And new business owners are commonly warned that after nine months or three years, they'll face enough roadblocks that they'll want to give up and shut things down.

But the people who simply accept these common views don't understand the power of the Ladder. Yes, any serious commitment is challenging. But those who know the steps of the Ladder can overcome such hurdles. They can turn every obstacle into increased successes.

Like all slumps, things like midlife crises or the so-called "seven-year itch" come with

> **Any serious commitment is challenging. But those who know the steps of the Ladder can overcome such hurdles. They can turn every obstacle into increased successes.**

both great opportunities for higher achievement and various temptations for whiny, escapist behaviors. In such slumps, as in every slump, the solution is the Ladder. Each rung is powerful and real.

For leaders, a midlife or post-midlife slump is a great call to significant improvement—if only they climb the rungs of the Ladder. In such times, refreshing your Dreams, Game Plan, and daily doses of great books and audios are lifelines to happiness.

On the other end of the scheduling spectrum, each day throughout your life has a foreseeable slump. Somewhere in the day, your energy will hit a low point and your enthusiasm will flag, if even just a little. Some cultures anticipate this and deal with it directly, with customs such as the *siesta* in Mediterranean culture or the English practice of tea time (and its famous spinoff, Tolkien's "second breakfast" of Hobbitish fame).

These planned rests and times of renewal at the dip of the day generally lead to more energy in the afternoon and an attitude of celebration almost every evening. Just when people in cultures without such traditions are exhausted and headed for bed, their counterparts in places such as Spain, Italy, and Latin America are ready for a fun evening with friends and family.

In fact, Western Civilization flourished at least in part because of the Biblical concept of a weekly Sabbath or sabbatical: a mini vacation held every week to keep the people renewed, refreshed, refocused, and revitalized. Similar traditions have proven the economic and societal value of holidays, athletic seasons and "off-seasons," summer vacations, and corporate retreats.

To adopt the wisdom of top leaders, learn from such examples and plan your next slump right now. Prepare your mini vacation, keep your written Dreams and Motivations updated and shiny, and write out your blueprint for each rung you'll climb next time you realize you're facing a slump.

Put the blueprint in a good place, somewhere you'll notice it daily, sitting there ready for use when the need comes. This habit doesn't increase the number of slumps that come (in fact, it will tend to reduce them), but it *will* make effective, immediate action the natural choice when any slump does arrive.

And, in truth, you may find yourself pulling out your blueprint and taking a powerful two-day mini vacation even when you aren't slumped at all! If this happens, embrace the Dream, and immerse yourself in excellent books, audios, and fun. You'll see the opportunities grow. That's exciting.

Even if no slump comes right now and causes you to look around and act on great opportunities, you can still climb the Ladder just for fun—because that's who you are, and you don't want to let any day go to waste.

> **Even if no slump comes right now and causes you to look around and act on great opportunities, you can still climb the Ladder just for fun—because that's who you are, and you don't want to let any day go to waste.**

This is a strategy for leaders, for the 5 percent. And when a slump does come, make sure your next blueprint is already sitting in that special place. Grab it, open it, and go to work!

No slump can beat the Ladder, not if you really engage and climb every rung.

> **When a slump does come, make sure your next blueprint is already sitting in a special place.**

So smile. You're ready. If a slump doesn't come, you know what to do. Climb the Ladder. Read and live your Dream and Game Plan. Every day. And if a slump does come, great. Grin. Chuckle. Laugh. A big opportunity is here! That's exciting. Now keep smiling. And climb the Ladder....

WORD OF THE DAY

vanguard: "forefront..., spearhead, front, front line, fore, lead, cutting edge; leaders, founders, founding fathers, pioneers..."

OPPOSITE: "rear"

(Compact Oxford Thesaurus)

NOTES

1   See C. S. Lewis, "The Inner Ring," *The Weight of Glory*.

2   Chris Brady, 2012, *A Month of Italy: Rediscovering the Art of Vacation*, 242.

3   Bill Lewis, "How to Handle Setbacks," audio, LIFE Leadership.

4   Robert Frost, "The Road Not Taken."

5   Claude Hamilton, "Pulling Out of a Slump," audio, LIFE Leadership.

6   Items in this section come from Claude Hamilton, "Pulling Out of a Slump," audio, LIFE Leadership.

7   Selections in this section are from Chris Brady and Orrin Woodward, *LIFE*, 74. Comments in [ ] are added to the original.

8   See, for example, Judith E. Glaser, *Conversational Intelligence*.

9   Chris Brady and Orrin Woodward, *LIFE*, 144.

10   Dan Hawkins, "Belief Is the Hardest Work You Will Do," audio, LIFE Leadership.

11   Trevor Cox, "Take Your Ears on Vacation," *Time*, March 24, 2014.

12   Ibid.

13   Chris Brady, 2012, *A Month of Italy: Rediscovering the Art of Vacation*, 322.

14   See Nassim Nicholas Taleb, *Antifragile: Things That Gain from Disorder*.

15   Ibid.

16   Ibid.

17   Ibid.

18   George Guzzardo, "Learn to Defeat the Decline," audio, LIFE Leadership.

19   See Graham Collier, "Escapism and Contemporary Life," *Psychology Today*, October 4, 2013.

20   Chris Brady, 2010, *Rascal: Making a Difference by Becoming an Original Character*, 98-100.

21   Claude Hamilton, "Pulling Out of a Slump," audio, LIFE Leadership.

22   See "The Four Stages of Escapism," *Daily Freedom* (online), July 2009.

23   Orrin Woodward, 2011, *RESOLVED: 13 Resolutions for LIFE*, 290-292.

24   Brian Tracy, 2010, *Goals!: How to Get Everything You Want — Faster Than You Ever Thought Possible*, v.

25   Ibid., 3.

Other Books in the
LIFE Leadership Essentials Series

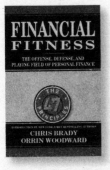

Financial Fitness: The Offense, Defense, and Playing Field of Personal Finance with Introduction by Chris Brady and Orrin Woodward

If you ever feel that you're too far behind and can't envision a better financial picture, you are so WRONG! You need this book! The *Financial Fitness* book is for everyone at any level of wealth. Just like becoming physically or mentally fit, becoming financially fit requires two things: knowing what to do and taking the necessary action to do it. Learn how to prosper, conserve, and become fiscally fantastic. It's a money thing, and the power to prosper is all yours!

Financial Fitness Workbook

Economic affairs don't have to be boring or stressful. Make managing money fun in a few simple steps. Use this workbook to get off to a great start and then continue down the right path to becoming fiscally fabulous! Discover exactly where all of your money actually goes as you make note of all your expenditures. Every page will put you one step closer to financial freedom, so purchase the *Financial Fitness Workbook* today and get budgeting!

Mentoring Matters: Targets, Techniques, and Tools for Becoming a Great Mentor with Foreword by Orrin Woodward

Get your sticky notes ready for all the info you're about to take in from this book. Do you know what it means to be a *great* mentor? It's a key part of successful leadership, but for most people, the necessary skills and techniques don't come naturally. Educate yourself on all of the key targets, techniques, and tools for becoming a magnificent mentor with this easy-to-apply manual. Your leadership success will be forever increased!

Turn the Page: How to Read Like a Top Leader with **Introduction by Chris Brady**

Leaders are readers. But there are many ways to read, and leaders read differently than most people do. They read to learn what they need to know, do, or feel, regardless of the author's intent or words. They see past the words and read with the specific intent of finding truth and applying it directly in their own lives. Learn how to read like a top leader so you'll be better able to emulate their success. Applying the skills taught in *Turn the Page* will impact your life, career, and leadership abilities in ways you can't even imagine. So turn the page and start reading!

SPLASH!: A Leader's Guide to Effective Public Speaking with **Foreword by Chris Brady**

For many, the fear of giving a speech is worse than the fear of death. But public speaking can be truly enjoyable *and* a powerful tool for making a difference in the lives of others. Whether you are a beginner or a seasoned orator, this book will help you transform your public speaking to a whole new level of leadership influence. Learn the SPLASH formula for great public speaking that will make you the kind of speaker and leader who makes a SPLASH—leaving any audience, big or small, forever changed—every time you speak!

The Serious Power of Fun with **Foreword by Chris Brady**

Life got you down? Feeling like life isn't much fun is a bad place to be. Fun matters. It is serious business and a source of significant leadership power. Without it, few people maintain the levels of inspired motivation and sustained effort that bring great success. So put a smile back on your face. Discover how to make every area of life more enjoyable and turn any situation into the right kind of fun. Learn to cultivate a habit of designed gratification—where life just keeps getting better—and *laugh your way to increased success* with *The Serious Power of Fun!*

Wavemakers: How Small Acts of Courage Can Change the World with Foreword by Chris Brady
Every now and then, extraordinary individuals come along who make huge waves and bring about permanent change in the lives of so many that society as a whole is forever altered. Discover from the examples of the various "Wavemakers" showcased in this book how you can make waves of your own and change the world for the better!

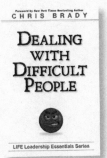

Dealing with Difficult People with Foreword by Chris Brady
How many times have you felt like banging your head against the wall trying to figure out how to deal with a routinely difficult person, whether at work or in your personal life? You can't control others, but you can control how you handle them. Learn about the seven main types of difficult people and the Five-Step Peace Process, and equip yourself to understand why people behave the way they do, break the cycle of frustration, and turn your interactions into healthy, productive experiences. "You are going to encounter difficult people. Plan on it. Prepare for it. Become good at it."

Financial Fitness for Teens: 6 Steps from Broke to Abundant with Foreword by Chris Brady
It's never too early to learn the principles of financial success. But schools often skip right over this crucial topic. And by the time many adults figure out that they don't know how to properly manage their money, they are often buried in debt and feeling helpless to dig themselves out. *Financial Fitness for Teens* aims to fill in the gap, break the cycle of bad financial habits and misinformation being passed down from generation to generation, and show youth how easy and exciting financial fitness can be. "The money thing" is one of the most important aspects of life to master—and the sooner, the better!

Conflict Resolution

Conflict Resolution is more than just reading words in a book. It's about utilizing what you learn in order to keep moving forward without negative baggage and drama. Tend to difficult situations properly, and instead of winning battles, you will win allies. This book will completely equip you to learn how to handle situations with grace, calmness, and strength. It takes courage to resolve conflict rather than to just run from it or ignore it. Your quality of life depends on it. With the right information, properly applied, your life can be peacefully productive.

Subscriptions and Products from
LIFE Leadership

Rascal Radio Subscription
Rascal Radio by LIFE Leadership is the world's first online personal development radio hot spot. Rascal Radio is centered on LIFE Leadership's 8 Fs: Faith, Family, Finances, Fitness, Following, Freedom, Friends, and Fun. Subscribers have unlimited access to **hundreds and hundreds** of audio recordings that they can stream endlessly from both the **LIFE Leadership website** and the **LIFE Leadership Smartphone App.** Listen to one of the preset stations or customize your own based on speaker or subject. Of course, you can easily skip tracks or "like" as many as you want. And if you are listening from the website, you can purchase any one of these incredible audios.

Let Rascal Radio provide you with **life-changing information to help you live the life you've always wanted!**

The LIFE Leadership Series
Here's where LIFE Leadership began, with the now famously followed 8 Fs: Family, Finances, Fitness, Faith, Following, Freedom, Friends, and Fun. This highly recommended series offers a strong foundation on which to build and advance in every area of your daily life. The timeless truths and effective strategies included will reignite passion and inspire you to be your very best. Transform your life for the better and watch how it will create positive change in the lives of those around you. Subscribe today and have the time of your LIFE!

Series includes 4 audios and 1 book monthly and is also available in Spanish and French.

The AGO (All Grace Outreach) Series
We are all here together to love one another and take care of each other. But sometimes in this hectic world, we lose our way and forget our true purpose. When you subscribe to the AGO Series, you'll gain the valuable support and guidance that every Christian searches for. Nurture your soul, strengthen your faith, and find answers to better understand God's plan for your life, marriage, and children.

Series includes 1 audio and 1 book monthly.

The Edge Series
You'll cut in front of the rest of the crowd when you get the *Edge*. Designed for those on the younger side of life, this hard-core, no-frills series promotes self-confidence, drive, and motivation. Get advice, timely information, and true stories of success from interesting talks and fascinating people. Block out the noise around you and learn the principles of self-improvement at an early age. It's a gift that will keep on giving from parent to child. Subscribe today and get a competitive *Edge* on tomorrow.

Series includes 1 audio monthly.

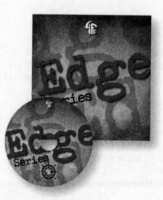

The Freedom Series Subscription (12 Months)

Freedom must be fought for if it is to be preserved. Every nation and generation needs people who are willing to take a stand for it. Are you one of those brave leaders who'll answer the call? Gain an even greater understanding of the significance and power of freedom, get better informed on issues that affect yours, and find out how you can prevent its decline. This series covers freedom matters that are important to *you*. Make your freedom and liberty a priority and subscribe today.

Subscription includes 1 audio monthly for 12 months.

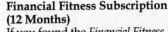

Financial Fitness Subscription (12 Months)

If you found the *Financial Fitness Pack* life-changing and beneficial to your bank account, then you'll want even more timely information and guidance from the Financial Fitness Subscription. It's designed as a continuing economic education to help people develop financial discipline and overall knowledge of how their money works. Learn how to make financial principles your financial habits. It's a money thing, and it always pays to be cash savvy.

Subscription includes 1 audio monthly for 12 months.

Financial Fitness Program

Once and for all, it's time to free yourself from the worry and heavy burden of debt. Decide today to take an honest look at your finances by learning and applying the simple principles of financial success. The *Financial Fitness Program* provides you with all the tools needed to get on a path to becoming fiscally fantastic!

Pack includes the Financial Fitness *book, a companion workbook, and 8 audio recordings.*

LLR Corporate Education Program

Based on the *New York Times* bestselling book *Launching a Leadership Revolution*, the LLR Corporate Education Program is designed not just to *train employees* but to *develop leaders*.

Leadership development is perhaps the single most important investment any company can make. *The leader creates the culture; the culture delivers the results.* So whether you're an employee, an HR manager, or a business owner, this course will benefit you. Enroll today and discover how to become a leader and your company's go-to person for solutions and performance. Or use the course to develop a whole team of go-to leaders and systemically create a permanent culture of leadership in your organization that impacts every employee and generates high morale, tremendous loyalty, and increased productivity!

Three 6-month courses are available. Subscribers can choose to subscribe for 6, 12, or 18 months. Each course includes 1 book and 4 audios monthly. Optional tests are included at no additional charge.